BUSH THEATRE

The Bush Theatre presents the world premiere of

The Herd

by Rory Kinnear

13 September – 26 October 2013
Bush Theatre, London

The Herd

by Rory Kinnear

Cast (in order of appearance)

Carol	**Amanda Root**
Claire	**Louise Brealey**
Patricia	**Anna Calder-Marshall**
Brian	**Kenneth Cranham**
Ian	**Adrian Rawlins**
Mark	**Adrian Bower**

Creative Team

Director	**Howard Davies**
Designer	**Helen Goddard**
Lighting Designer	**Rick Fisher**
Sound Designer	**Mike Walker**
Casting	**Hancock Stevenson Casting**
Company Stage Manager	**Kate Wilson**
Assistant Stage Manager	**Claire Louise Baldwin**
Assistant Stage Manager (placement)	**Remi Bruno Smith**
Production Electrician	**Nic Farman**
Costume Supervisor	**Claire Wardroper**
Set Builder	**Footprint**
Production Carpenter	**Rebecca McWalter**

The Bush would like to give thanks to: Mac Cosmetics, Royal Court, Tricycle Theatre, Playful Productions, Chris Harper, Notting Hill Prep School, Alain Airth and Lauren Clancy at AKA, Caroline Gardner, Tracks, Daisy Chain Gift Company, Hampstead Theatre, National Theatre, Radio Times, Stage Electrics, White Light, Talking Tables and the *Independent*.

Adrian Bower Mark

Theatre credits include *Ordinary Dreams* (Trafalgar Studios); *Hedda* (Gate); *Elling* (Bush Theatre/Trafalgar Studios); *The Hotel in Amsterdam* (Donmar Warehouse); *In Celebration* (Chichester Theatre); *Mister Heracles* (West Yorkshire Playhouse); *Brassed Off* (National Theatre); *Romeo and Juliet* (Chester Gateway); *The Knocky* (Royal Court); *Ballad of Wolves, Silverface* (Gate); and *Julius Ceasar* (Royal Exchange).

Television credits include *A Touch of Cloth, Mount Pleasant, Rev, Monroe, Outcasts, Harry and Paul, Lennon Naked, Runaway, Apparitions, Talk to Me, The Quartermass Experiment, The Inspector Lynley Mysteries, Faith, Dirty Filthy Love, The Hotel in Amsterdam, Teachers, Badger, Gimme Gimme Gimme, In Your Dreams, Dangerfield, The Heart Surgeon,* and *Supply and Demand*.

Film credits include *Hard Boiled Sweets, The Waiting Room, A Performance* and *Jude*.

Louise Brealey Claire

Theatre credits include *The Trojan Women* (Gate); *Birthday, The Stone and Sliding with Suzanne* (Royal Court); *Sixty-Six Books* (Bush); *Government Inspector* (Young Vic); and *Uncle Vanya* and *Little Nell* for the Peter Hall Company.

Television credits include *Sherlock, Hotel Babylon, Mayo* and *Bleak House*.

Film credits include *The Best Exotic Marigold Hotel* and *Delicious*.

Anna Calder-Marshall Patricia

Theatre credits include the season of *Weekly Rep, Death Tax, Untitled Matriarch Play, In the Republic of Happiness, Objections to Sex & Violence, Uncle Vanya* (Royal Court); *Salt, Root & Roe* (Donmar Trafalgar Season); *A Kind of Alaska, Tejas Verdes* (Gate); *Comfort Me with Apples, Formation Dancers, Dear Janet Rosenberg, While the Sun Shines* (Hampstead); *Humble Boy* (Gielgud); *A Lie of the Mind* (Donmar Warehouse); *Antigone* (Old Vic); *The Secret Rapture* and *The Devil is an Ass* (National Theatre); *The Philistines* and *Too Good to be True* (RSC).

Television credits include *Laurence Olivier Presents King Lear, Stage Door Johnnies, 13 Steps Down, New Tricks, Poirot, Dalziel & Pascoe, Midsomer Murders, The Prince in Love, Lovejoy, Heartbeat, Sherlock Holmes, Witness Against Hitler, Strife, Inspector Morse, Strangers & Brothers, Days, Bloomers, Matilda's England, Under Western Eyes, Two Days in the Life of Michael Reagan, Colombe, Male of the Species* for which she won an Emmy Award.

Film credits include *Wuthering Heights, Anna Karenina, Zulu Dawn* and *Madame Curie*.

Kenneth Cranham Brian

Cranham's career spans over thirty years working in film, television and theatre.

Theatre credits include The Inspector in *An Inspector Calls* (National Theatre, West End and Broadway) for which he was nominated for an Olivier Award for Best Actor. A leading man at the Royal Court from 1966–1983 he performed in major plays by Orton, Bond and Pinter including *The Birthday Party* in which he played Stanley to Harold Pinter's Golberg. Other theatre credits include *The Homecoming* (Almeida).

Film credits include *Layer Cake*, *Oliver*, *Made in Dagenham* and the soon to be released *Closed Circuit* and Disney's *Maleficent* with Angelina Jolie.

Adrian Rawlins Ian

Theatre credits for the Bush Theatre include *The Clearing* and *The Maiden's Prayer*.

Other theatre credits include *The Miser, Her Naked Skin, Tons of Money, A Small Family Business, A View from the Bridge* (National Theatre); *The House of Special Purpose* (Chichester); *The Glass Menagerie* and *Good* (Manchester Royal Exchange); *Easter* (RSC); *Hamlet* (Riverside); and *Clever Dick* (Hampstead).

Television credits include *Silent Witness, Prisoners' Wives, Mrs Biggs, Law & Order, The Old Curiosity Shop, Lewis, Dunkirk, May Day, Marple, Clapham Junction, Bouquet of Barbed Wire* and *Doctor Who.*

Film credits include the *Harry Potter* films, *Breaking the Waves, The Raven, The Railway Man* and *Wilbur Wants to Kill Himself.*

Amanda Root Carol

Theatre credits include *Jumpy* (Royal Court and the West End); *The Norman Conquests* (Old Vic and Broadway) for which she received a Tony Award nomination; *Conversations after a Burial* (Almeida); *The Deep Blue Sea* (Chichester) and extensive work with the RSC including *Love's Labour's Lost, Troilus and Cressida, The Seagull, The Man of Mode, The Constant Couple* and *Macbeth*.

Television credits include *The Forsyte Saga, Mortimer's Law, Anna Karenina, Law & Order, A Touch of Frost, Foyle's War, Rose and Maloney, Empire, The Robinsons, Fiona's Story, Love Again* and *Daniel Deronda.*

Film credits include *The Iron Lady, Whatever Happened to Harold Smith, Persuasion* and *Jane Eyre.*

Rory Kinnear Playwright

The Herd is Rory's debut play.

As an actor, Rory Kinnear has worked with the Royal Shakespeare Company, Almeida Theatre, Donmar Warehouse and the National Theatre. In 2010 Kinnear played Angelo in *Measure for Measure* at the Almeida Theatre, and later the title role in *Hamlet* at the National Theatre. The two roles won him the Best Actor award in the Evening Standard Theatre Awards. He also won an Olivier Award and the Ian Charleson Award for his performance of Sir Fopling Flutter in *The Man of Mode* at the National Theatre.

Other theatre credits include *The Revenger's Tragedy*, *Philistines*, and the role of Mitia in a stage adaptation of the Nikita Mikhalkov film *Burnt by the Sun* (National Theatre). He is currently playing Iago in the National's production of *Othello*, directed by Nicholas Hytner.

Television credits include *Southcliffe, Count Arthur Strong, Loving Miss Hatto, The Mystery of Edwin Drood, Black Mirror: National Anthem, Richard II* and *Cranford*.

Film credits include *Skyfall* and *Broken* for which he won Best Supporting Actor at the British Independent Film Awards.

Howard Davies Director

Howard Davies is an Associate Director of the National Theatre, and was previously Associate Director for the Almeida Theatre and RSC. Davies established and ran the Warehouse Theatre for the RSC where he directed and produced twenty-six new plays in four years.

He received Olivier and Evening Standard Awards for Best Director for his production of *The White Guard*. His other recent National Theatre productions also include *The Last of the Haussmans, The Cherry Orchard, Blood and Gifts, Burnt by the Sun, Gethsemane, Her Naked Skin, Never So Good, Philistines* and *The Life of Galileo*.

As well as theatre both in London and New York, Davies has directed opera, television and film.

Helen Goddard Designer

Helen graduated from Bristol Old Vic Theatre School and was a winner of the Linbury Biennial Prize for Stage Design in 2007.

Theatre credits include *A Doll's House* (Manchester Royal Exchange; *Proof* (Menier Chocolate Factory); *Werther* (Scottish Opera); *The Country Wife* (Royal Exchange); *Steel Magnolias* (David Ian Productions, UK tour); *Romeo and Juliet* (Headlong); *Dublin Carol* (Donmar Trafalgar Season); *The Village Bike* (Royal Court); *Dream Story, Lulu* (Gate); *Lake Boat* (Arcola); *The Years Between* (Northampton Theatre Royal); *Comedians, Looking for Buddy* (Bolton Octagon); *And a Nightingale Sang* (New Vic/touring); *James and the Giant Peach* (Watermill); *The Ones that Flutter, The Lifesavers* and *GBS* (Theatre503); *Knives in Hens* (Ustinov Studio Bath); *Let There Be Love* (Tricycle); *Lovely and Misfit* (Trafalgar Studios) and *The Roaring Girl* (Bristol Old Vic Studio).

Rick Fisher Lighting Designer

Rick is the winner of two Olivier Awards for Best Lighting Design and two Tony and Drama Desk Awards, for *Billy Elliot* and *An Inspector Calls* (Broadway).

Recent work includes *Great Expectations* (Bristol); *Raving* (Hampstead); *Inside Wagner's Head* (Linbury, Royal Opera House). Recent theatre includes *Othello* (Singapore); *Heather Gardiner* (Birmingham Rep); *The Audience* (Gielgud); *Galileo, Richard III* (RSC); *Judas Kiss* (Duke of Yorks); *Old Money, 55 Days, Farewell to the Theatre* (Hampstead); *Chariots of Fire* (Hampstead/Gielgud); *Hero* (Royal Court); *Twelfth Night* (Singapore); *Way of the World* (Sheffield). Previous work includes *The Merchant of Venice* (RSC); *Sweeney Todd* (Chatelet, Paris); *The Sound of Music* (Buenos Aires); *Tribes, A Number* (Royal Court); *Billy Elliot, the Musical* (West End/Australia/Broadway/US tours); *An Inspector Calls* (West End); *Jerry Springer the Opera, Blue/Orange* (National Theatre/West End); *Much Ado About Nothing* (Singapore); *Family Reunion, Betrayal, The Philanthropist, Old Times* (Donmar Warehouse) and *Far Away* (New York).

Opera credits include *The Tsarina's Slippers* (Royal Opera); *Die Entführung aus dem Serail, Maometto Secondo* (Garsington); Theodore Morrison's *Oscar* and *La Grande-Duchesse de Gérolstein, Les Pêcheurs de Perles, Madama Butterfly, Albert Herring, Wozzeck* (Santa Fe); *Turandot* (ENO); *Peter Grimes* (Norwegian National Opera); *Der fliegende Holländer* (Vilnius); *Turandot* and *The Fiery Angel* (Bolshoi); and *Heart of Darkness* (ROH2, Linbury Studio Theatre).

Mike Walker Sound Designer

Mike first worked at the Grand Theatre, Wolverhampton, before training at The Guildhall School of Music and Drama in London.

UK theatre credits include *Home, Hymn (Untold Stories), St Matthew Passion, Caroline or Change, Major Barbara, Jerry Springer – The Opera* (for which he won the first Olivier Award for Best Sound Design) and *Carousel* (National Theatre); *Disgraced, Mammals, How Love is Spelt* (Bush); *Dear World, Hay Fever, Crazy for You, Lord of the Flies, The Glass Menagerie, Into the Woods, The Fantasticks!, Eurobeat, Saucy Jack and the Space Vixens, Hello Dolly!, Gigi, Bat Boy – The Musical, Jus' Like That , The Full Monty, The Graduate, Oliver!* (West End and London); *Certified* (Leicester); *Arturo Ui* (Chichester); *The Three Musketeers* (Kingston); *Stop Dreamin'* (Windsor); *Peter Pan* (Leeds); *Aspects of Love* (tour), *Amadeus* (Sheffield); *Time's Up!* (Guildford).

Singapore theatre credits include *Othello, Twelfth Night, Macbeth, Much Ado About Nothing, Avenue Q, Midsummer Night's Dream, Cabaret, My Fair Lady, Forbidden City, Honk!, Chang and Eng, They're Playing Our Song, M Butterfly, Art, A Twist of Fate, Hamlet, Sing to the Dawn, Little Shop of Horrors, Noye's Fludde, Kampong Amber, Death of a Salesman, Into the Woods.*

Mike, with his company Loh Humm Audio, provides sound design, engineering and installation services for theatres.

Gemma Hancock CDG & Sam Stevenson CDG Casting

Previous work with Howard Davies includes *Blood and Gifts* (NTO); *55 Days* (Hampstead). Casting for other theatre includes *King Lear* (tour for the RSC); *The Humans* (international tour); *Our Country's Good* (UK tour and St James Theatre); *In the Club*, *Abigail's Party*, *What the Butler Saw*, *Everything is Illuminated* (Hampstead); *Henry IV, Parts 1 & 2*, *The Portrait of a Lady*, *A Doll's House*, *The Vortex* (also West End), *Pygmalion* (also Old Vic), *Little Nell*, *Amy's View*, *Habeas Corpus*, *Measure for Measure*, *You Never Can Tell*, *Waiting for Godot*, *Much Ado About Nothing*, *As You Like It*, *The Dresser*, *Man and Superman*, *Happy Days*, *Miss Julie*, *Private Lives*, *Blithe Spirit*, *Don Juan*, *Betrayal* (Theatre Royal Bath); *Where There's a Will*, *Uncle Vanya*, *Canary* (ETT); *The Deep Blue Sea* (tour and West End); *Tejas Verdes*, *The Emperor Jones*, *The Chairs* (Gate, Notting Hill); *Watership Down* (Lyric Hammersmith); *Alice's Adventures in Wonderland*, *Beasts and Beauties* (Bristol Old Vic); *Breakfast at Tiffany's*, *Waiting for Godot*, *Ring Round the Moon* (West End).

Recent work for television includes *The Selection*, *Nightshift*, *Care*, *The Snipist*, *Nixon's the One*, *The Minor Character*, four series of *Silent Witness*, *Money*, *Consuming Passion*, *The Inspector Lynley Mysteries*, and *The Bill*. Gemma and Sam received a Primetime Emmy nomination for their casting of *Emma* for BBC1.

Recent film work includes *Private Peaceful* and *Leave to Remain*.

BUSH THEATRE

The Bush Theatre is a world-famous home for new plays and an internationally renowned champion of playwrights and artists. Since its inception in 1972, the Bush has pursued its singular vision of discovery, risk and entertainment from a distinctive corner of West London. Now located in a recently renovated library building on the Uxbridge Road in the heart of Shepherds Bush, the theatre houses a 144-seat auditorium, rehearsal rooms and a lively café-bar.

The Bush Theatre, 7 Uxbridge Road, London, W12 8LJ
Box Office: 020 8743 5050 Administration: 020 8743 3584
email: info@bushtheatre.co.uk
The Alternative Theatre Company Ltd (The Bush Theatre) is a registered charity and a company limited by guarantee. Registered in England No. 1221968. Charity No. 270080

THANK YOU TO OUR SUPPORTERS

The Bush Theatre would like to extend a very special Thank You to the following Star Supporters, Corporate Members and Trusts & Foundations whose valuable contributions help us to nurture, develop and present some of the brightest new literary stars and theatre artists.

LONE STAR
Anonymous
Eric Abraham
Gianni Alen-Buckley
Michael Alen-Buckley
Steffanie Brown
Siri & Rob Cope
Jonathan Ford & Susannah Herbert
Catherine Johnson
Miles Morland
Lady Susie Sainsbury
James & Virginia Turnbull
John Paul Whyatt

HANDFUL OF STARS
Anonymous
David Bernstein & Sophie Caruth
Micaela & Christopher Boas
Francois & Julie Buclez
Philip & Tita Byrne
Clyde Cooper
Irene Danilovich
Catherine Faulks
Lyn Fuss
Simon & Katherine Johnson
Emmie Jones
Paul & Cathy Kafka
Nicolette Kirkby
Pierre Lagrange & Roubi L'Roubi
Adrian & Antonia Lloyd
Eugenie White
  & Andrew Loewenthal
Scott & Laura Malkin
Peter & Bettina Mallinson
Charlie & Polly McAndrew
Aditya Mittal
Paige Nelson
Georgia Oetker
Laura Pels
Bianca Roden
Naomi Russell
Joana & Henrik Schliemann
Philippa Seal & Philip Jones QC
Larus Shields
The van Tulleken family
Trish Wadley
Charlotte & Simon Warshaw
Hilary & Stuart Williams

RISING STARS
ACT IV
Nicholas Alt
Anonymous
Melanie Aram
Nick Balfour
Todd Benjamin & Sonja Shechter
John Bottrill
Jim Broadbent
David Brooks
Lord & Lady Burlington
Maggie Burrows
Clive Butler
Matthew Byam Shaw
Benedetta Cassinelli
Tim & Andrea Clark
Claude & Susie Cochin de Billy
Carole & Neville Conrad
Matthew Cushen

RISING STARS CONTINUED
Andrew Duncan
Charles Emmerson
Jane & David Fletcher
Lady Antonia Fraser
Sylvie Freund-Pickavance
Vivien Goodwin
Jack Gordon & Kate Lacy
Kate Groes
Hugh & Sarah Grootenhuis
Thea Guest
Lesley Hill & Russ Shaw
Bea Hollond
Ingrid Jacobson
Ann & Ravi Joseph
Davina & Malcolm Judelson
Kristen Kennish
Nicola Kerr
Sue Knox
Caroline Mackay
Isabella Macpherson
Michael McCoy
Lady Thalia McWilliam
Judith Mellor
Caro Millington
Kate Pakenham
Kevin Pakenham
Denise Parkinson
Mark & Anne Paterson
Julian & Amanda Platt
Peggy Post
Barbara Prideaux
Radfin Courier Service
Emily Reeve
Joanna & Michael Richards
Robert Rooney
Claudia Rossler
John Seal and Karen Scofield
Justin Shinebourne
Saleem & Alexandra Siddiqi
Melanie Slimmon
Brian Smith
William Smith-Bowers
Nick Starr
Jack Thorne
Jan & Michael Topham
Ed Vaizey
Marina Vaizey Francois
  & Arrelle von Hurter
Amanda Waggott
Olivia Warham
Peter Wilson-Smith & Kat Callo
Alison Winter

CORPORATE MEMBERS

SPOTLIGHT
John Lewis, Park Royal
Walt Disney & Co Ltd

FOOTLIGHT
Innocent

LIGHTBULB
The Agency (London) Ltd
Markson Pianos
RPM Ltd

SPONSORS & SUPPORTERS
Kudos
MAC
Ogilvy & Mather
The Groucho Club
Waitrose Community Matters
Westfield
West 12 Shopping
  & Leisure Centre

TRUSTS AND FOUNDATIONS
The Andrew Lloyd Webber
  Foundation
Coutts Charitable Trust
The Daisy Trust
The D'Oyly Carte Charitable Trust
EC&O Venues Charitable Trust
The Elizabeth & Gordon Bloor
  Charitable Foundation
Foundation for Sport and the Arts
Garfield Weston Foundation
Garrick Charitable Trust
The Gatsby Charitable Foundation
The Goldsmiths' Company
Hammersmith United Charities
The Harold Hyam Wingate
  Foundation
Japan Foundation
Jerwood Charitable Foundation
The J Paul Getty Jnr Charitable
  Trust
The John Thaw Foundation
The Laurie & Gillian Marsh
  Charitable Trust
The Leverhulme Trust
The Martin Bowley Charitable Trust
The Theatres Trust
The Thistle Trust
Sir Siegmund Warburg's Voluntary
  Settlement
Sita Trust
The Williams Charitable Trust
The Worshipful Company of
  Grocers Settlement

PUBLIC FUNDING

Supported by
ARTS COUNCIL ENGLAND

supported by

hammersmith & fulham

If you are interested in finding out how to be involved, please visit the 'Support Us' section of www.bushtheatre.co.uk, email development@bushtheatre.co.uk or call 020 8743 3584

THE HERD

Rory Kinnear

Characters

CAROL, *mid-fifties, Andy's mother*
CLAIRE, *thirty-three, Andy's sister*
PATRICIA, *late seventies, Andy's grandmother*
BRIAN, *late seventies, Andy's grandfather*
IAN, *late fifties, Andy's father*
MARK, *late thirties, Claire's boyfriend*

The play is set in the downstairs kitchen and living room of a suburban house.

Note on Text

A forward slash (/) indicates an overlap in speech.

Dialogue in square brackets [] is unspoken.

This text went to press before the end of rehearsals and so may differ slightly from the play as performed.

The front room of a suburban house. An adjoining kitchen and living/dining room. Stairs leading to an unseen second floor. A corridor to a bathroom. A downstairs bedroom off the living room. The room is cursorily decorated for a birthday party.
CAROL, *mid-fifties but young, is on her home phone, perched on a living-room armchair, busily wrapping some presents.*

CAROL. And is he in the bus?... He *is*?... And you're in the bus with him?... How?... How are you in the bus with him?... They mended it today, did they?... Mended, fixed... Right, but *yesterday* Jackie said it was still broken... Evening... Right, so *not* mended then. So if the cordless phone isn't working how are you talking to me in the bus?... Right. So if you're not, is Andy?... Murat, you promised me he would be ready to leave by eleven thirty... No it's not, it's twelve... It is... Murat, it's twelve o'clock and you are still faffing about... Faffing, I can't [think of another word]... Wasting time... Have you got his jacket on at least?... His jacket, Murat, you must know what 'jacket' is, his coat?... Yes? And are his drugs all there?... All of them, are you sure?... The Colomycin?... Because last time you forgot it...

CLAIRE, *thirty-three, lets herself in the front door.*

CLAIRE. People over the road, their car lights are... oops, sorry...

CAROL (*mouthing to* CLAIRE). Two minutes. (*On phone.*) Are they there in front of you?... Yes? Can you slowly read out the names of all the drugs in his bag?... (*To* CLAIRE.) Pitta breads, in the freezer.

CLAIRE. Car lights? Shall I say something?

CAROL (*ignoring her*).... Yes, well, he's already late, isn't he? Okay. So... What?... Sorry, can you spell it?... Fee? Is that V?... Yes?... V... E... N... Right, Ventolin... Yes, Ventolin... Yes, that is how you say it. Next one... Oh God, Murat, that sounds like nothing on earth...

CLAIRE (*having placed the pitta breads on the kitchen sideboard*). I'm going to pop round and let them know.

CAROL (*ignoring her*)....Listen, Murat, can I speak to Jackie? It's probably going to be quicker... No, Jack-IE, jack-ET was earlier but well remembered... yes, and will you please, please, please get Andy into the bus now... Thank you... Yes, Jackie, thank you... The *lovely* Jackie... (*To* CLAIRE, *absentmindedly.*) Did you find them?... (*Sees the pitta breads.*) Can you... (*Notices she's not in the room and calls out to her.*) Claire, can you pop the pitta breads in the microwave to defrost please? And make a salad dressing? I've got to speak to the lovely Jackie... without vomiting... Claire?... Claire, are you there?... Are you in the toilet?... (*To phone.*) No sorry, Jackie, not you... Yes, I just want to make sure he's got all his drugs for the weekend... I know, I just wanted to make absolutely sure, after last time... No, I'm not blaming anyone... Sure, but to be sure... Great, can you read out all the drugs there in Andy's bag? Thank you... Ventolin, yes, Colomycin, Atrovent, yes...

CLAIRE *re-enters*.

CLAIRE. There's no answer.

CAROL. What?

CLAIRE. There's no answer over the road.

CAROL (*on phone*). Sorry, Jackie, just... (*To* CLAIRE.) What's over the road?...

CLAIRE. The new couple. Are they away?

CAROL. I don't think so... (*On phone.*) Sorry, my daughter's... (*To* CLAIRE.) Hang on... (*On phone.*) Sorry, yes, I'm ready... Undivided... Great... great... great... (*To* CLAIRE.) Defrost... (*On phone.*) Great, all of them?... and the Nutrison?... how many bottles?... Lovely... fine, okay, wonderful. And Murat's getting him in the bus now, is he?... Great... yes, hope so... Just his grandparents and his sister, and some friends of mine... I'm sure it will be... about an hour and a bit then... I'm sure it will be, bye then. (*Hangs up.*)

If she says it *once* more, I swear. 'How lovely.' What is lovely, Jackie, what actually is lovely? Like a fucking parrot.

CLAIRE. The people over the road. Their car lights are on.

CAROL. What?

CLAIRE. I'll pop over later, see if they need any help.

CAROL. Oh God, you don't have to worry about them. Wouldn't piss on you if you were on fire.

CLAIRE. It's alright, I'll just pop over…

CAROL. Honestly, they're ghastly.

CLAIRE. Wouldn't you appreciate…?

CAROL. Oh, don't take the moral high ground, for God's sake. I've jump leads in the boot if they need them. Did you make the dressing?

CLAIRE. You didn't ask.

CAROL. I did.

CLAIRE. When?

CAROL. Earlier.

CLAIRE. You didn't.

CAROL. Yes I did, Claire.

   Oh, no, you weren't in the toilet.

CLAIRE. What?

CAROL. Can you?

CLAIRE. What?

CAROL. Make a dressing?

CLAIRE. Yes. Can you calm down?

CAROL. Claire… make it a request or a command, don't make it a question when it's quite obvious that's the last thing on my mind. I've got your grandfather and your brother…

CLAIRE. Fine. You. Are Going. To Calm. Down.

   CLAIRE *begins to make the dressing as* CAROL *moves to the kitchen and decants an orange-juice carton into a jug.*

CAROL. Actually shaking. How does she do it?

CLAIRE. Who?

CAROL. Who do you think?

CLAIRE. Don't obsess. It won't help if you…

CAROL. How can I not obsess? If someone made you feel like a piece of shit every time you spoke to them, what would you do?

CLAIRE. Not speak to them.

CAROL. Yes, Claire. I don't have that luxury.

It's not actually that she makes me feel like a piece of shit because I honestly think she makes everyone feel like a piece of shit. Her little sneer would make Nelson Mandela feel like a piece of shit. I don't mind being made to feel like a piece of shit. I'm good at it. What gets me, what I really can't *stand* is the 'Mrs Griffith'. She has never called me Carol…

CLAIRE. I know.

CAROL.…not once. I have screamed at her, I've cried on her, I've been in a room with her studiously ignoring Andy's erection…

CLAIRE. Mum!

CAROL.…but she has never dared to call me Carol. 'Mrs *Griffith*… how *lovely*, Mrs *Griffith*… I think you'll find you're wrong, Mrs…' each one's like a papercut on the eye.

CLAIRE. You could always change it?

CAROL. It's not the *Griffith* that bothers me.

CLAIRE. No?

CAROL. No! Of course… What bothers me is I know that if she called me Carol she'd have to recognise me as a human being. And she can't do that because then she'd have to treat me like one. She'd have to return my calls and understand when I'm worried and maybe even sometimes smile in the right places and little by little she'd be forced to realise that the reason that once upon a time I had been given a name was that I was a Real Person.

Ever called me Carol she'd fall to pieces. Throw her arms around me and beg for forgiveness. So no, she is resolute. No Carols for her...

No wonder she makes them have a multi-faith Christmas service.

CLAIRE. I'm not sure they call it Christmas in a multi-faith service.

CAROL. Pedant.

CLAIRE. Racist.

Do you want me to lay the table?

CAROL. I'll do it.

CAROL *begins to lay the table for four people.*

CLAIRE. Is he on his way?

CAROL. So they say.

CLAIRE. How was he in the end?

CAROL. Still a bit wheezy.

CLAIRE. Did the doctor come out?

CAROL. No, they said they didn't want to call the doctor out because he'd come out for Louis the night before.

CLAIRE. So?

CAROL. So... they didn't want to, they actually said this, they felt if it wasn't serious they didn't want to inconvenience him.

CLAIRE. By asking him to see a patient?

CAROL. Yes, they must find it awfully boring, doctors. Seeing all these ill people, when they could be doing something fun. Like paragliding.

CLAIRE. What's Louis got to do with Andy anyway?

CAROL. Well quite. But there you are, it was a boat I didn't feel like rocking.

CLAIRE. That's awful. They can't just make one client's health...

CAROL. Oh God, Claire.

CLAIRE. What?

CAROL. Don't call Andy a client.

CLAIRE. Seriously, Mum.

CAROL. Well, *seriously*, this *primary carer* didn't want a *client's* birthday to be ruined.

CLAIRE. They don't think like that.

CAROL. They do.

CLAIRE. That's ridiculous. They wouldn't put a kid's health at risk just because they found a parent annoying. Imagine if we did that at school.

CAROL. Think of the class sizes.

CLAIRE. I'm trying it from now on, don't worry.

They don't actually though, do they?

CAROL. I wouldn't be surprised. I'm sure it would give them great pleasure. To punish him because of me.

Anyway, they said he was a lot better this morning, which was annoying.

CLAIRE. Why?

CAROL. To hear their satisfaction.

CLAIRE. Dangerous, Mother.

CAROL. I joke, of course.

Will you get me down four wine glasses?

CLAIRE *does so.*

CLAIRE. Didn't you say some people were coming?

CAROL. Sorry?

CLAIRE. On the phone.

CAROL. What?

CLAIRE. Are they coming later?

CAROL. What are you talking about?

CLAIRE. On the phone. You said some friends were coming.

CAROL. What? Oh God, yes.

CLAIRE. What?

CAROL. Yes, not entirely true.

CLAIRE. What do you mean?

CAROL. I lied I'm afraid.

CLAIRE. You lied?

CAROL. High ground…

CLAIRE. Why?

CAROL. Claire, that woman can patronise people to death. If she knew only his grandparents and sister were coming for his twenty-first birthday, her drone of pity might very nearly have killed me. I'd more than likely have had a pity-induced stroke. You'd have found me on the floor, eyes lolling, wonky mouth, saying over and over 'but I don't mind'.

CLAIRE. So no one else is actually coming?

CAROL. No, darling. Put me on the pyre and strike the match: I am a liar.

CLAIRE. Oh.

CLAIRE *hands* CAROL *the glasses*.

CAROL. Don't give me the disapproving face.

CLAIRE. It's not a face. It's a…

CAROL. What?

CLAIRE. I just thought.

CAROL. What?

CLAIRE. It might have been nice.

CAROL. Come on, your grandmother's still coming, how much fun can you want?

CLAIRE. No, not that… just…

CAROL. What?

CLAIRE. Well, is it alright if… well, would there be room for anyone else?

CAROL. Er, I suppose so, who is it?

CLAIRE. I don't think you know them.

CAROL. Them? I've only the one lasagne.

CLAIRE. No, it's just one.

CAROL. Oh. Who is it?

CLAIRE. You don't know them.

CAROL. Are 'they' coming for lunch?

CLAIRE. I think so.

CAROL. Why didn't you tell me before?

CLAIRE. They didn't know if they could make it.

CAROL. Well, who is it?

CLAIRE. Just… he's called Mark.

A moment.

CAROL. Mark?

CLAIRE. Yes.

A moment.

CAROL. A new friend?

CLAIRE. No.

CAROL. A close friend?

CLAIRE. Yes, reasonably.

CAROL. An old friend, newly close?

CLAIRE. Stop it, Mum. He's a friend.

CAROL. Fine.

A special friend?

CLAIRE. Mum...

CAROL. It's okay to ask, isn't it? If he's coming into my house.
To meet my family. If he's wanting to do that it's not too
much of a leap to think he might be a special friend...

CLAIRE (*snorting*). Special friend...

CAROL. Well?...

CLAIRE. He wants to meet Andy, that's all.

CAROL. Right.

I'll go and change.

CLAIRE. No...

CAROL *leaves, upstairs*.

The doorbell rings. CLAIRE *answers*. PATRICIA,
mid-seventies, enters.

Hiya, does he need a hand?

PATRICIA. Please. (*Handing her a covered cake tin*.) Could
you take this as well?

CLAIRE. Certainly. How was the drive?

CLAIRE *takes the cake tin and puts it down in the kitchen*.

PATRICIA. Fine, darling. Have you got the base?

CLAIRE. I have.

PATRICIA. He'd kill us both.

CLAIRE. I'll get him.

CLAIRE *goes out the front door.*

PATRICIA (*calling up*). Carol, we're here. You'll be delighted
to learn that the cake has made it. We had to tell the taxi not
to go over twenty-five and to slow down to five around
corners. Your father was delighted. It was like a hearse.

I thought people were going to start lining the streets.
Waving it off.

Carol?

CAROL (*emerges, checks, whispers*). Claire's bringing someone…

PATRICIA. Really? *Someone* someone?

CAROL. Not sure. Maybe.

PATRICIA. Is there anything I can do?

CAROL. Just sit. Talk to Claire.

PATRICIA. Right. I'll be discreet.

CAROL. And I'll believe you. (*Heads back up the stairs.*) Dad's cushion's under the sink…

CLAIRE *and* BRIAN *enter.* BRIAN, *late seventies, walks with heavy reliance on a walking stick.*

CLAIRE. That's it. Almost in. Crikey, you put on weight?

BRIAN. Very heavy coat. Had a look at it yet?

CLAIRE. Not yet. I carried it to the kitchen but I haven't…

BRIAN. You had it by the base?

CLAIRE. I certainly did. I made it all the way. It's over there, just waiting for us.

BRIAN. To hack it to pieces.

CLAIRE. I know.

BRIAN. Barbarians.

CLAIRE. I could frame it if you'd prefer.

BRIAN. Don't tempt me.

PATRICIA. Having your cake has always been enough for your grandfather.

CLAIRE *and* BRIAN *have arrived in front of the armchair.*

Your mother said his cushion's under the sink.

CLAIRE. Great, will you take him…

PATRICIA *supports her husband whilst* CLAIRE *gets his pillow.*

You're looking well, Granddad.

BRIAN. Not bad, love, not bad at all.

PATRICIA. How's Andy?

CLAIRE. Alright. He was a bit wheezy last night but he seems better this morning. Mum, on the other hand...

CLAIRE *goes to look in the covered cake tin.*

PATRICIA. What about her?

BRIAN. No peeking, now.

CLAIRE. Touchy, isn't he, oh she's getting obsessed again about this Head of Home.

PATRICIA. This Jackie?

CLAIRE. Yes. Seems to think it's becoming personal.

PATRICIA. Isn't that good? Everything else these days seems to be going the other way.

CLAIRE. Personal as in vindictive, I'm afraid. Okay, Picasso, one, two, three and... sit.

CLAIRE *and* PATRICIA *help* BRIAN *into an armchair.*

There you go.

BRIAN. I wouldn't eat a cake Picasso had made...

CLAIRE. Do you want a drink, either of you?

BRIAN. ...probably make the icing out of beef. / A tea would be lovely, angel.

PATRICIA. / An Earl Grey if you have, Claire.

CLAIRE. Won't be a minute.

She goes to the kitchen and fills the kettle.

PATRICIA. Do you think she's right?

CLAIRE. What?

PATRICIA. Jackie. Is she as awful as your mother says she is?

CLAIRE. I don't know. *I* don't like her.

PATRICIA. Why's that?

CLAIRE. Oh, you know, works with the disabled so thinks she's Jesus.

BRIAN. Holier-than-thou, is she?

CLAIRE. Yeah, the fifty grand a year slightly undermines the sermons though.

Having put the kettle on, CLAIRE *returns to the sitting room.*

How's the Shakespeare going, Granddad?

BRIAN. *Love's Labour's Lost* this month. Bloody boring. But they do nice biscuits.

PATRICIA. Oh yes, it's the biscuits you go for.

CLAIRE. What's that?

PATRICIA. Your grandfather has the distinction of being the only man in the class. He assures me from accident rather than design. I imagine it wouldn't matter what they were studying. It might be the entire back catalogue of *TV Quick* and he'd come home with a smile on his face.

Is your mother okay? She's been very snappy on the phone.

CLAIRE. I don't know. She's been a bit weird.

Last weekend she cried when she found a dead bird.

PATRICIA. Carol?

CLAIRE. I know. We went for a walk in the park and...

PATRICIA. A dead bird?

CLAIRE. Yes, by a tree.

PATRICIA. Oh, how wonderful. Did she pick it up?

CLAIRE. No, she didn't pick it up, she just sort of stood over it and... well, started crying. Just a bit, I mean she wasn't bawling... but... then she... sort of..

PATRICIA. What?... Oh, Claire, please say she said a prayer... please!...

CLAIRE. No, God, she's not that far gone… but she mouthed something like…

PATRICIA. Like what?

CLAIRE. Well, I don't know for sure but it sounded like 'bless you'.

BRIAN *and* PATRICIA *laugh.*

BRIAN. Sneeze to death, did it?

PATRICIA. Oh, Claire, this is serious. Crying at a dead bird. Your mother loathes animals.

CLAIRE. I know she does, I know, but I think… I think she saw this bird and there was no one around it and no one cared that this bird had lived or died and I think she thought…

PATRICIA. Oh Claire, that's ridiculous.

CLAIRE. I know it's not true. I know how loved Andy is.

All I'm saying is that recently she's been low.

PATRICIA. Well, what about you? A new boyfriend, I hear.

CLAIRE. What? I knew this… I was only outside for a minute.

PATRICIA. You know your mother.

CLAIRE. Yes, that's why…

BRIAN. That's lovely, Claire. Is he nice?

CLAIRE. Granddad, he's… It's not… A friend of mine is coming over today, that's all. It's not…

BRIAN. What does he do?

CLAIRE. Why does that matter?

PATRICIA. So that when your friend comes over, we've something to talk about.

CLAIRE. Because you've always found conversation difficult.

PATRICIA. How long have you…?

CLAIRE. Grandma, please. Don't.

PATRICIA. Claire, we're happy.

CLAIRE. I'll call him and tell him not to come. Just, please, don't push it.

PATRICIA. Alright, Claire, don't…

CLAIRE. Promise me?

PATRICIA. Claire, I'm far too old to promise. But I assure you I shall be discreet.

CLAIRE. Please.

PATRICIA. Enough.

BRIAN. Is the kettle boiled?

CLAIRE. Sorry, Granddad. I'll do it.

She goes to the kitchen.

BRIAN. Fifty, sixty years ago, of course, they'd have just been locked away. You've got to say that's progress.

CLAIRE. Yes, I know. I suppose we're lucky in some ways. Just… doesn't feel like luck, though.

BRIAN. Luck. It could be you.

CLAIRE. What do you mean?

BRIAN. The Lottery. It could be you.

CLAIRE. Granddad, don't say that.

BRIAN. Not you, I mean anyone. Could be anyone. Bad luck. Good luck, it's all chance. Rotten sort of lottery though. Life.

PATRICIA. Plato. Aristotle. Brian.

The home phone rings. CLAIRE *answers it.*

CLAIRE. Hello?… Yes, is that Jackie?… Sure, I'll just get her… Mum!… Mum, it's Jackie…

PATRICIA. Is everything okay?

CLAIRE. Yeah, she just wants a word with Mum.

CAROL comes down and picks up the phone.

CAROL. Hi?… Great… / And his chest?… Right, well Murat's got the nebuliser there with him, hasn't he?… I will but until he is with us he is still your responsibility // so shouldn't you call him as well to see that he knows what to do… I do… Jackie, I like Murat an awful lot but sometimes his English isn't great… Thank you… /// Yes, I will too… Yes, it's next Tuesday, isn't it?… Oh great… great that's a lot easier… Why?… No, absolutely not. No… No, it's his birthday, we've family //// and friends here who want to spend time with him. I want to spend time with him, not with a nutritionist… ///// I can't believe you're doing this… Well it feels on purpose… Right, do you have her number?… collect////// Of course I want to change it… Yes, just text it to me… fine, bye.

BRIAN. / What we got for lunch?

CLAIRE. Lasagne.

BRIAN. Ooh lovely, Italian.

PATRICIA. // I see what you mean.

CLAIRE. You think this is bad.

/// How was the concert?

BRIAN. Oh, wonderful, Claire, wonderful. They did this arrangement of this song by this band, what were they called, Patricia?

PATRICIA. I haven't the faintest…

BRIAN. Well, it was really raspy. And the chap playing the solo was a character. Had a bowtie. With fish on it.

CLAIRE. //// One minute, Granddad.

///// No, Mum…

////// Oh no. She can't…

CAROL *puts the phone down.*

CAROL. Un-fucking-believable.

BRIAN. What is it?

CLAIRE. Sit down, Mum.

CAROL. That woman.

PATRICIA. What was it?

CAROL. Andy's nutritionist… I can't believe she would… Andy's nutritionist is going away for a month, which we all knew, so we'd brought forward his review by a week but now her daughter has a driving test that day which she wants to be with her for so she's said she can only make it today.

CLAIRE. A driving test?

CAROL. I know. Even if it *is* true it's hugely fucking insulting.

CLAIRE. What are you going to do?

CAROL. I'm going to phone her and have an argument I imagine, darling, because that would appear to be what I do. It is my calling.

PATRICIA. And she wants to come here?

CAROL. Yes. What a lovely surprise.

BRIAN. Poor old Andy.

CAROL. Quite, Dad. Can you imagine, his twenty-first birthday?

BRIAN. I know. He'll be expecting a stripper.

CAROL. Hi, Dad, anyway. Hello, Mum. How's the Shakespeare?

BRIAN. *Love's Labour's Lost*.

PATRICIA. Not for want of trying.

The sound of a text message arriving.

CAROL. Ah, thank you, Jackie.

If it means washing her hands of something she's out of the blocks like a… like a…

She is looking around the sitting room.

Oh God, darling, have you seen my mobile?

CLAIRE. No, have you had it today?

CAROL. Erm, I don't know…

CLAIRE. Is it in your jacket? It sounded like it was in your…

CAROL (*it is*). Oh, Carol, you are an idiot… thank you… I'll do this upstairs… There may be blood…

She goes upstairs. PATRICIA *pointedly stares at* CLAIRE.

CLAIRE. What?

PATRICIA. She can't do it like this any more, Claire. She looks awful.

CLAIRE. What can I do, Grandma?

PATRICIA. Her hair looks dry, her skin… She's pushing herself too hard.

BRIAN. She's strong, Patricia. She's always been strong.

PATRICIA. Well it can't go on. She's still got a chance to be happy in life. I don't want her to throw away that chance for… well, for Andy.

CLAIRE. Grandma.

PATRICIA. She has to meet people, make more friends.

BRIAN. And how does she do that?

PATRICIA. What, have you never met people? Through societies, through clubs…

BRIAN. Carol? Carol doesn't do packs.

PATRICIA. Well, she can go to the cinema. To a restaurant.

BRIAN. By herself?

CLAIRE. Grandma, I have tried.

PATRICIA. Well, could you not just help her…?

CLAIRE. What do you think I do?

PATRICIA. Let me finish. Could you not just help her a little bit…

CLAIRE. Excuse me, I go up to see him every third week. When he comes home I'm here almost every night, please don't insinuate that I could be doing more. We could all be doing more.

BRIAN. She's not saying that, Claire, we're just worried.

CLAIRE. You have no idea of… I can't just give my life over to… You can't say that. We all love him but, please, I'm thirty-three, I'd like a life too.

BRIAN. We know, Claire, we know, she's sorry.

PATRICIA. I wasn't suggesting you ruin your life, Claire. We've already said how pleased we are about your boyfriend…

CLAIRE. Don't talk about Mark.

PATRICIA. Oh, for goodness' sake, Claire, it's a good thing.

CLAIRE. Please don't.

PATRICIA. Don't be angry. You should be…

CLAIRE. You promised you wouldn't.

PATRICIA. I didn't.

CLAIRE. Yes you did.

BRIAN. She assured, Claire.

CLAIRE. Whatever it was, she lied.

PATRICIA. I did not lie to anyone.

BRIAN. She assured, Claire. Not promised. It turns a lie into just a disappointment.

A text message arrives on CLAIRE*'s mobile, in the kitchen. She goes to get it.*

PATRICIA. But we have a name at least.

BRIAN. Patricia, yellow card. Calm down or you'll be off.

Did we ever get our tea?… Claire?

CLAIRE (*reading her text message*). Sorry?

BRIAN. Our tea?

CLAIRE. I'll be with you in a minute.

She puts her hand on the kettle.

PATRICIA. Is it from Mar…?

CLAIRE. I swear, I will pour this on your legs

CAROL *re-enters*.

CAROL. Right. Fuck you, Jackie. The meticulous fucking planning…

PATRICIA. What?

CAROL. She can't do any other day for the next six weeks. She has to come today.

CLAIRE. / Oh God.

BRIAN. / Can't it wait?

CAROL. No.

BRIAN. What's the problem?

CAROL. He's putting on weight, he needs new intake levels. I just want to fucking scream.

BRIAN. Oh, love.

PATRICIA. What time will she be here?

CAROL. Well it was two but I got it up to four.

Right. What time did you say your friend was coming?

CLAIRE. He's, er… he's just texted, he's getting into the station.

CAROL. Oh, is he come on the train?

CLAIRE. Er, yep.

CAROL. Where from?

CLAIRE. What does that matter?

CAROL. I'm just asking where his train is coming in from, Claire.

CLAIRE. From Brighton… he's coming in from Brighton.

PATRICIA. Brighton? Oh wonderful, where ambition goes to die.

CLAIRE. Mum… Mum, please tell the woman that bore you: she's beginning to bore me too.

PATRICIA. Oh, very good, Claire.

CAROL. Discreet, were you, Mum?

PATRICIA. I stayed within the boundaries.

CAROL. That you set yourself.

A car is heard outside. CLAIRE *goes to the window.*

Is that him?

CLAIRE. No, it's a taxi. I think it's the people opposite. I'll see if they need those jump leads. Car keys?

CAROL. In the basket.

CLAIRE. Thanks.

CAROL. My pleasure.

CLAIRE *leaves.*

Will you two be okay? I'll be five minutes.

PATRICIA. I think we'll manage. We have met before.

CAROL *goes back upstairs.*

Did you hear her?

BRIAN. When?

PATRICIA. When Carol asked her if it was him?

BRIAN. And?

PATRICIA. And she said it wasn't.

BRIAN. Because it wasn't.

PATRICIA. No. She said 'No, it's a taxi.'

BRIAN. So?

PATRICIA. As if it couldn't possibly be him if it was a taxi.

BRIAN. Meaning what?

PATRICIA. That Mark couldn't afford to take a taxi. Even when he's meeting his girlfriend's family for the first time.

BRIAN. Patricia…

PATRICIA. Come on, Brian. Brighton? You're the Graham Greene fan.

BRIAN. Patricia, I am not talking about this man until I have met him and made my own mind up. Okay? My *own* mind.

Is the cake alright?

PATRICIA. No, it's grown wings and flown into a puddle.

BRIAN. Very funny, help me up.

PATRICIA. It's fine, stay there.

BRIAN. I need to go to the bathroom. Help me up.

PATRICIA. Oh, are you sure?

BRIAN. Just help me up.

PATRICIA. Fine, one moment... one, two, three. Up... There's your stick. Have you got it?

BRIAN. Yes.

PATRICIA. Careful of the table.

BRIAN. Not blind.

PATRICIA. And you're certain you need to go?

BRIAN. As Christopher Columbus said, my darling, I won't know for sure until I get there.

PATRICIA. Idiot.

BRIAN. That's why you love me. I pale beside you.

They both go into the toilet.

Did we get our tea?

The door closes after them.

A moment.

The doorbell rings.

CAROL (*off, from upstairs*). Mum!

Silence.

It rings again.

(*Off.*) Mum, can you get that please?

PATRICIA (*off*). I'm in the bathroom with your father, Carol.

CAROL (*off*). Mum!

She comes down the stairs.

Mum, did you not hear? Mum?

PATRICIA (*off*). I'm in here with your father, Carol. I won't be long.

CAROL. Oh. I think it's him.

PATRICIA (*off*). Well, can you wait a minute?

CAROL. I can't do that, Mum. It's rude.

PATRICIA (*off*). Carol, I don't want to meet him coming out of a toilet.

CAROL. Well, hurry up.

BRIAN (*off*). It's no good rushing me.

The doorbell rings.

CAROL. Mum, I'm sorry. I've got to let him in.

PATRICIA (*off*). Fine.

BRIAN (*off*). Always made a good first impression.

CAROL (*laughs*). Just make sure you wash your hands.

She goes to the door, hesitates, then returns to the bathroom door and whispers.

It is Mark, isn't it?

PATRICIA (*off*). Yes.

CAROL. I had a mad rush and thought it might be Matthew. Right. Well, good luck, everybody.

She returns to the door and opens it.

IAN. Hi.

Pause.

CAROL. What the fuck do you want?

Silence.

IAN. I'd like to see Andy. To give him his birthday present.

CAROL. He's not here.

IAN. Will he be?

CAROL. Yes.

IAN. Well, can I wait for him?

CAROL. Sure.

She shuts the door on him.

The doorbell rings. She ignores it.

PATRICIA (*off*). Carol? Carol, did you get it?

CAROL. Yes.

CAROL *goes to the sofa and sits down.*

PATRICIA *enters, alone.*

PATRICIA (*looking around, whispering*). Where is he?

CAROL. It wasn't him.

PATRICIA. Oh. Who was it?

CAROL. It wasn't him.

PATRICIA. Oh. I'll let your father out then.

PATRICIA *goes back into the bathroom. There is a flush of the toilet.*

They both re-emerge, PATRICIA *leading* BRIAN.

BRIAN. False alarm, was it?

CAROL. Yes, Dad.

BRIAN. Who was it?

A moment.

CAROL. It was Ian.

Silence.

PATRICIA. Where is he?

CAROL. I told him to wait until Andy got here.

PATRICIA (*whispering*). What, is he outside the door?

CAROL. I think so.

BRIAN. Claire'll see him, won't she?

CAROL. She is allowed to.

PATRICIA. Yes but she doesn't. She won't want to.

BRIAN. I'll go and talk to him.

CAROL. No, Dad, don't.

PATRICIA. What does he want?

CAROL. He said he wanted to give Andy his birthday present.

A moment.

PATRICIA. Did he have one?

CAROL. What?

PATRICIA. A birthday present. Did he have a birthday present with him?

CAROL. Why does that...?

PATRICIA. Well, I can take the present from him and he can leave.

BRIAN. It's not about the present, Patricia.

CAROL. I can't believe this.

PATRICIA. Really? Does anything surprise you about him?

(*Looking out the window.*) I can't see him.

BRIAN. Love.

CAROL. Mum, get down. Just... pretend we're not here.

PATRICIA. I know he's stupid...

CAROL. Just come and sit down. Dad, here sit down... one... two... three...

They are all sat.

PATRICIA. Carol, listen to me. This is not to ruin Andrew's birthday. He is not to come here and hijack what you've done...

CAROL. It's a lasagne Andy can't even eat, Mum.

PATRICIA. I don't just mean today. He is not to come in here, all smiles, and make the rest of us have to...

CAROL. We don't...

PATRICIA. Carol, be quiet. You know what'll happen. He will take over, think he's charmed us all and then skip back to his new life saying thank God that's all over.

CAROL. Mum, it's not about him, is it?

PATRICIA. What?

CAROL. It's Andy's birthday, Mum.

I want him to be happy.

PATRICIA. And he will be. So let's not mention it and we'll have a happy time and forget all about it.

CAROL. It's Andy's birthday and seeing his father might make him happy.

A moment.

PATRICIA. You don't seriously... Carol, this is not just about Andy.

BRIAN. We all want Andy to have a lovely day, you know that. Yes, he *might* like it...

PATRICIA. And he might not...

BRIAN....but you and Claire won't. It'll be horrible for the pair of you. And Andy might even pick up on that, so no one's the winner.

PATRICIA. Except him.

CAROL. Andy doesn't understand what he's done, Dad. Who knows what he thinks. He might love to see him.

PATRICIA. He won't remember him.

CAROL. He might, Mum. You can't say that for sure. He is his father.

PATRICIA. You call that being a father?

CAROL. No, but this isn't about what I think of him. Or you. This is about what Andy might think.

PATRICIA. Andy? Think? Oh very New Age. Listen, if it's going to make you happy…

CAROL. Amazingly I'm not thinking about myself.

PATRICIA. Well honestly, I don't know what you're thinking…

CAROL. I'm thinking that this might be the last time Andy gets to see his father.

Because what they do share is the ability to make me think, whenever I say goodbye to either of them, that I might not ever see them again.

A moment.

BRIAN. I don't think that's genetic.

CAROL. No, but it keeps you on your toes.

CLAIRE *enters.*

CLAIRE. What an arsehole.

CAROL. What?

CLAIRE. I practically had to beg him for a thank-you. I found myself standing there, like I was waiting for a tip. Annoyingly his car was fine.

CAROL. Yes… Yes, I told you. And they say Dutch people are meant to be friendly.

PATRICIA *has gone to the window. She turns back to* CAROL *and shakes her head.*

CLAIRE. Are they Dutch? I thought they were from Liverpool.

A text message sounds.

CAROL. Was that mine or yours?

CLAIRE. Yours… Is it upstairs? I'll get it.

CAROL. No, don't worry. I'm… I'm going to change.

CLAIRE. Mum… Please don't go to any extra effort. You don't have to… He's very relaxed.

CAROL. I'm not changing for your friend, Claire.

CLAIRE. Oh really.

CAROL. Yes, really. It's got colder.

She leaves.

CLAIRE. And she's off to her room again. She's like a teenager. Oh God, your teas.

She resumes making them.

PATRICIA. Oh, don't worry.

BRIAN. Hallelujah!

PATRICIA. Brian, she's not our slave. Sit down, Claire.

CLAIRE. It's alright.

Silence.

PATRICIA. That's nice he's relaxed.

CLAIRE. What?

PATRICIA. Mark, that's nice he's nice and relaxed.

CLAIRE. I'm not even rising to it, Grandma.

She brings over their teas.

Here you are. Mind you don't burn your mouth.

BRIAN. Good things come to those who wait, eh?

CLAIRE. That better be about the teas.

They are all sat.

Silence.

PATRICIA. I wonder what the Dutch for 'thank you' is?

CLAIRE. Mmn?

PATRICIA. The Dutch. For 'thank you'.

CLAIRE. I don't know.

A moment.

PATRICIA. Brian?

BRIAN *stares pointedly for a long time at his flailing wife.*

BRIAN (*after some time*). Shanksh?

A moment.

PATRICIA. Your hair is looking lovely today, Claire. Isn't it, Brian?

BRIAN. Everything will look lovely if someone will please pass me my tea.

CLAIRE *passes the tea to* BRIAN.

CAROL *enters. She is wearing a different, prettier blouse.*

CAROL. It was Murat. They're stuck in traffic. At least I presume that's what troffac is.

PATRICIA. What a *pretty* blouse, Carol.

A moment.

CAROL. Thank you, Mother.

CLAIRE. What's wrong with you today?

PATRICIA. Mmn?

The doorbell rings.

CLAIRE. Right, if possible, will you please act normally.

PATRICIA. I'll get it, darling.

CLAIRE. Hands off.

CAROL. Will you help your grandfather up first?

CLAIRE *and* BRIAN. What?

PATRICIA. Oh yes, darling, can you? To rearrange him? / His pillow. It gets… // He doesn't like to ask in front of strangers.

BRIAN. / I don't need rearranging.

CLAIRE. // Now?

CLAIRE. Quickly then. (*To* PATRICIA.) Don't you dare…
Come on, Granddad, up we go… / one… two… three…

BRAIN. / Please don't treat me like…

With BRIAN *lifted, supported by* CAROL *and* CLAIRE,
PATRICIA *opens the door and goes outside.*

CLAIRE. Grandma, don't you…!

PATRICIA (*off*). Oh, hello?

MARK (*off*). Er, hi… is… is Claire there?

CLAIRE. Come in, Mark… one… two… three…

MARK *enters as* BRIAN *is sat down, somewhat
haphazardly.*

MARK. Hi.

CLAIRE. Hi. You found it alright?

MARK. Yeah, yeah.

They kiss, a little awkwardly.

CLAIRE. Sorry about… Er, this is my granddad Brian, my
mum Carol. This is Mark.

CAROL. Hi, Mark. Lovely to erm… Lovely to… (*Looking at
the door and* PATRICIA, *still outside*.) Mum?

Is everything alright, Mum?

Mum?

PATRICIA *re-enters.*

PATRICIA (*pointedly*). Fine. Everything's fine.

CLAIRE (*to* MARK). Sorry.

PATRICIA. Mark, how lovely to meet you. I'm Patricia,
Claire's grandmother. We've heard so much about you. Can
we get you anything to drink. A tea? Or a beer?

MARK. Ooh, I don't know, it's a bit early for that. I'll just have
a glass of water, please.

PATRICIA. Oh, you're from the North?

A moment.

MARK. How'd you tell?

BRIAN. Women's intuition, Mark.

CAROL. Fizzy?

MARK. Please.

CLAIRE. From Lancaster.

BRIAN. Like the Bombers!

MARK. Yeah, that's right.

PATRICIA. But Claire said you were coming up from Brighton.

MARK. That's right, that's where I live now.

CLAIRE. They are allowed to travel.

MARK. That's right – as long as we've got our passports.

BRIAN. And had your tests.

MARK (*laughs*). Watch it.

BRIAN *laughs*.

A moment as the laughter subsides.

PATRICIA. Oh. How lovely.

CAROL. Here's your water.

MARK. Thank you. I brought this. For yourself. And this. For the birthday boy.

CAROL. Oh, that's very kind. Thank you. Sit down, will you?

CLAIRE. How was the train?

MARK. Yeah, fine, fine.

BRIAN. Bet you're used to it by now, heh?

MARK. What's that?

BRIAN. The journey.

MARK. Yeah, yeah, kinda.

Silence.

PATRICIA. It's lovely to meet you.

MARK. Thank you. You too.

A moment.

It's a lovely place / you've got here.

PATRICIA. / And what is it you do, / Mark?

CAROL. / Are you hungry, Mark?

MARK (*to* CAROL). I could be. (*To* PATRICIA.) Sorry?

PATRICIA. And what is it you do?

CAROL (*sotto*). Mum.

MARK. I'm, er… I'm a poet.

Silence.

PATRICIA. A poet?

CAROL. Here's some pitta breads.

MARK. Yeah, 'mongst other things.

PATRICIA. A poet as in writing poems?

A moment.

MARK. Yep.

CAROL. And I'll get some dips. Mum, a hand?

PATRICIA *and* CAROL *move to the kitchen*.

CLAIRE. Mark does performance poetry.

BRIAN. That sounds fun. What does that do?

CLAIRE. He goes to clubs and bars and festivals and performs his poems in front of an audience. Live. It's really popular.

BRIAN. Really?

CLAIRE. Yeah, really. It's like being a musician.

MARK. But with words.

CLAIRE. He's like a rock star, Granddad.

MARK. Without the groupies.

BRIAN. You have to say that, do you?

PATRICIA. And do you publish?

MARK. Sorry?

PATRICIA. As well as read them out. Do you publish them?

MARK. That's the idea.

CLAIRE. He's got hundreds.

PATRICIA. So you do write them down?

MARK. Yeah.

CLAIRE. He reads them out of this huge book.

MARK. Some I make up on the spot. Improvise.

CAROL. Really? That must be daunting.

MARK. Only if you've got nothing to say.

PATRICIA. And does that ever happen?

MARK. Hardly ever, touch wood.

CAROL. There's something you've got in common, Mum.

A text message goes, upstairs.

Sorry, will you excuse me, Mark?

CLAIRE. Just leave it down here.

CAROL *goes upstairs.*

BRIAN. She'll wear herself out with the stairs alone.

CLAIRE. She's scared of carrying her mobile on her. She thinks she'll get cancer of the leg.

MARK. Ah well, she might be proved right.

CLAIRE. Rather defeats the point of having one, though.

MARK. What, a leg?

BRIAN. I've found they're rather overrated.

CAROL (*off*). I'm going to be five minutes.

CLAIRE. Is everything alright?

CAROL (*off*). Just going to have a little shout at Murat.

CLAIRE. Very good.

PATRICIA *brings over dips*.

PATRICIA. That's Claire's brother's carer, Murat. His English is a little… annoying.

MARK. Right.

PATRICIA. Has Claire told you about Andy?

MARK. Yeah, yeah, a lot.

PATRICIA. He is very disabled.

MARK. Yeah, I know, yeah.

CLAIRE. No, I missed that bit out.

PATRICIA. Well, I know some people find it difficult to talk about.

MARK. No, s'alright. I had a cousin who was…

PATRICIA. Oh really, what did he have?

MARK. Oh, she was Down's syndrome.

PATRICIA. Oh, I'm sorry. Andy is a lot worse than Down's.

A moment.

BRIAN. I think that's what one calls a pyrrhic victory, Mark.

PATRICIA. Claire's mother has had to bring him up single-handedly as well.

MARK. Claire said.

PATRICIA. I mean, we've all done what we could. But it was a very difficult time, awful, when Claire's father left. He hurt them all enormously.

CLAIRE. Alright, don't terrify the man.

PATRICIA. Claire was seventeen. But little Andrew was only five.

MARK. Five? Right, right… Poor chap.

PATRICIA. Exactly.

A moment.

MARK. Is it *twelve* years then between you?…

CLAIRE. Well…

MARK. I thought it was ten.

CLAIRE. No, they're just…

BRIAN. Claire's been like another mother to Andy, she has.

PATRICIA. Oh, she's been wonderful. We'd all be at sea without her.

BRIAN. And here he is. Still soldiering on. Defying them all. Doctors said he wouldn't make it past nineteen – didn't reckon on the Wilkinson family fighting spirit.

MARK. Nineteen? Oh… oh right.

A moment.

Sorry, I thought it was his twenty-first for some reason. That's rather ruined the card.

PATRICIA. Sorry?

MARK. I'd just… I'd done a poem. In his card.

PATRICIA. How is that ruined?

MARK. I thought it was his twenty-first.

BRIAN. But it…

CLAIRE. It doesn't matter.

PATRICIA. Darling?

CLAIRE. It doesn't matter… Nineteen or twenty-one, I'm sure the sentiment will be the same.

An uncomfortable silence as PATRICIA *and* BRIAN *begin to understand.*

PATRICIA. And how is your little cousin doing?

MARK. Oh, I'm afraid she passed away.

CAROL *re-enters, brandishing her mobile.*

CAROL. Right, see, I'm bringing it down. And I'm leaving it here.

BRIAN. Take his punishment like a man, did he?

CAROL. Oh, it was fine. Sorry, Mark, for dashing off like that, it was Andy's carer. Do you know what he put in his text message? 'Very much coughing.' That was it. Like that's not going to make you think the worst.

PATRICIA. Andy has a very bad chest.

CAROL. Yes, sorry, Mark, very boring, medical stuff but… Andy and his carer are coming in the bus they've got at his home, which he loves, but it can make him laugh and that can make him wheezy so… we have to be careful. Anyway I called him and, yes, he's a bit wheezy but he wasn't coughing. Certainly not 'very much'.

CLAIRE. How wheezy?

CAROL. He's a bit crackly but… I tell you they think I'm overprotective, as soon as they're alone and in charge they shit themselves. Excuse my language, Mark…

MARK. Please, don't mind me.

CLAIRE. Will he be alright?

CAROL. I don't know, probably. I told Murat to give him his nebuliser in the van, we'll see. We might have to do some physio on him when he gets here.

CLAIRE. I'll get his pillow out.

CLAIRE *goes into Andy's room.*

CAROL. I am sorry, Mark. We're rather throwing you into the thick of it here. I'd love to say it's not always like this but when Andy's over it all gets a little chaotic.

MARK. You think this is chaos, I live in Brighton.

CLAIRE (*off*). Mum, where is it?

CAROL. In the cupboard.

But he did say the troffac has cleared up. So we might eat on time.

PATRICIA. How long have you lived in Brighton, Mark?

MARK. Nearly twenty years, now. Yeah, went to university down there and just seemed to stay.

PATRICIA. Oh, university?

CAROL. Not lost the accent though?

MARK. No. There're a few of us down there, I'm afraid to say.

BRIAN. Friends from home?

MARK. Yeah, and picked up along the way. Tend to police each other a bit. Make sure those vowels stay nice and flat.

BRIAN. I say tomato and you say – (*Lancashire*.) tomahhhto.

MARK. You say potato and I say chips.

CLAIRE *re-emerges*.

CLAIRE. Right, do you want to have the tour?

MARK. Oh, okay, grand.

CAROL. Don't go into my room, it's a shitheap.

MARK. It's alright, I won't judge you, I promise.

CAROL. Yes, but if you're not disgusted I might judge you.

CLAIRE. Fine, we'll give it a wide berth.

They leave upstairs.

A moment.

CAROL. Do you think he just won't come back?

PATRICIA. I have no idea. But there's nothing you can do.

CAROL. This is ridiculous. I have to tell Claire.

PATRICIA. If he comes back she'll know. If he doesn't, what was the point of upsetting her.

CAROL. I can't believe he'd...

PATRICIA. Carol, it is not in your control.

CAROL. I don't even have his number any more. I can't even call him.

Isn't that awful? I don't even have his number any more.

PATRICIA. Why would you need it?

CAROL. Because much as we might like to ignore the fact, we have two children together.

PATRICIA. A fact he has *studiously* ignored.

A moment.

CAROL. I should put the lasagne in.

She does so.

He seems nice. Normal. I have to say my heart sank when he said...

PATRICIA. I know, darling. We both covered ourselves exceptionally.

I think we might have a *little* problem.

CAROL. Oh no really? Why, what did he say?

PATRICIA. No, nothing, no, not... I think your daughter might be taking after her mother a little.

CAROL. How?

PATRICIA. Well, I happened to mention the age gap between Claire and Andrew. That it was twelve years.

CAROL. And?

PATRICIA. And, well, that seemed to make him think that that made it Andrew's nineteenth birthday.

A moment.

CAROL. Why?… Oh, no… Really?… Claire, you little…
(*Laughs*.) Oh poor Claire… Oh hang on, no, what about my
card? It says 'Happy Twenty-first' on it.

PATRICIA. Well in that it would appear you are not alone.
Maybe it would be best if we left the card-openings until
after he's left.

CAROL. Claire, you little… well, the cheeky little liar.

PATRICIA. Glass houses, Carol.

CAROL. Two years, really. Is it worth it?

PATRICIA. It certainly adds an unnecessary excitement to the
day.

BRIAN. Would anybody mind if I had a quick half-hour?

CAROL. No, Dad, course not.

BRIAN. Just before the birthday boy gets here.

CAROL. Do you want to lie on Andy's bed?

BRIAN. Yep. Get me out the way.

CAROL. Mum, a hand?… One… two… three.

BRIAN. Stick.

CAROL. There you are.

PATRICIA. Right. Onwards.

They move off toward the bedroom.

BRIAN. It's a marble cake, Carol.

CAROL. Is it? That sounds nice.

BRIAN. Not easy, I can tell you. Not easy at all.

CAROL. I'm sure we'll appreciate it.

BRIAN. Butter icing too. Chocolate.

PATRICIA. Nobody likes a show-off.

As they enter the bedroom.

BRIAN. And the top is emblazoned with 'Happy Twenty-first
Andrew'.

CAROL. Oh, Dad, no…

The door shuts.

A moment.

CLAIRE *and* MARK *re-emerge down the stairs.*

CLAIRE.…and I made them time me.

MARK. You spoilt…

CLAIRE. I know, I was awful.

MARK. Why time you though?

CLAIRE. Because I could. Only child then.

A moment.

This is stupid.

MARK. Claire.

Silence.

Where've they gone?

CLAIRE. Probably putting Granddad down.

MARK. What, just because he's old?

CLAIRE *laughs.*

Pause.

CLAIRE. It's idiotic.

MARK. Claire, I want to be here. I want to.

A moment.

You feeling alright?

CLAIRE. Okay.

MARK. Nothing today, no?

CLAIRE. No. It's been fine.

Pause.

MARK. You don't want me to leave, do you?

CLAIRE. No, no.

A moment.

It's not like I could put it off much longer.

MARK. That's nice.

CLAIRE. You know what I mean.

MARK. I hope so.

CLAIRE. Yeah.

Pause.

MARK. I do know it's still your decision. / I'm not projecting anything I promise just… Please know though that… I'm not going to let you down.

CLAIRE. / Thanks for the responsibility.

Mark…

MARK (*interrupting her*). No, just let me, please… this is what I think. I'm not sure it even has to mean anything to you. I'd like it to but… But to me… this is the happiest I've ever been…

CLAIRE. You mean it's all downhill from here then?

MARK. Fuck me, you make it hard for yourself sometimes.

CLAIRE. Sorry.

MARK. I mean, I think it would be absolutely wonderful. So… no pressure. That was a joke.

CLAIRE. I know. Thank you.

That means… I mean, it's a lot, means a lot… to me too. But I am… I mean, it's… I am scared.

MARK. Jesus Christ, *you're* scared? I've just met your grandmother.

Look, I will be here. If you want me, this… Alright?

CLAIRE. I know. That's… thanks.

MARK.
> 'Darest thou now, O soul,
> Walk out with me toward the unknown region
> Where neither ground is for the feet nor any path to
> follow?'

CLAIRE. That's unfair.

MARK.
> 'I know it not, O soul,
> Nor dost thou, all is blank before us,
> All waits undream'd of in that region, that inaccessible
> land.'

CLAIRE. Did you write…?

MARK. It's Walt Whitman.

They kiss.

The doorbell rings.

CLAIRE. Aha, is this our guest of honour? Now you get to see what the fuss is about.

CLAIRE opens the front door as CAROL enters from the bedroom.

CAROL. Claire!

IAN (*holds a bloody tissue to his mouth*). Hi.

CLAIRE. What the fuck do you want?

A moment.

IAN. Claire, can I just come in, I've…

CAROL. What's happened?

CLAIRE. Mum!

IAN. It's fine. I've… I've split my lip. Is it alright if I…?

CLAIRE. No, you can't.

CAROL. Claire, let him in.

CLAIRE. Absolutely not.

CAROL. Claire, just...

CLAIRE. No.

CAROL. What happened?

IAN. It was an accident.

CLAIRE. I don't care. What are you doing here?

CAROL. I'll get you some TCP.

CLAIRE. Mum, don't you dare. He knows where the bathroom is.

IAN. Can I come in then?

CLAIRE. No! What are you thinking? How dare you just come here?

CAROL. Claire, just let him... Don't bleed on the carpet.

CLAIRE. I don't believe this.

IAN. Thanks.

CLAIRE. You do *remember* where the bathroom is, don't you?

IAN. Yes, Claire. Look, I'm sorry. I'll... I'll just... Clean myself up...

IAN *goes to the bathroom.*

CLAIRE. Mum, what are you...?

CAROL. He came earlier. When you were over the road.

CLAIRE. What?! Why didn't you...?

CAROL. I did, I told him to piss off. I didn't think he'd come back.

CLAIRE. When's he ever taken any notice of what anyone says?

CAROL. I guess, I guess you're right.

CLAIRE. What's he done to himself?

CAROL. I don't know. That's a new development.

CLAIRE. Jesus.

MARK. I take it that's your dad?

CLAIRE. Yes.

CAROL. I'm sorry, Mark. Yes. It's Claire's father. And we're not together any more, I'm sure you know. And, er... it's a bit of a surprise... to see him.

CLAIRE. Of course he'd come today. You should read the birthday cards he sends me. They're desperate.

PATRICIA *enters*.

PATRICIA. Was it him?

CAROL. Yes.

CLAIRE. What!?

PATRICIA. Has he gone?

CAROL. He's in the bathroom.

CLAIRE. Was *anybody* going to tell me?

PATRICIA. Why's he in the bathroom?

CAROL. He's split his lip.

PATRICIA. Oh Carol, really. Pathetic.

CLAIRE. Thanks a lot. I'm not staying here if he's here.

CAROL. Claire, don't be angry with me. I didn't invite him.

CLAIRE. Then just tell him to leave.

CAROL. Andy is going to be here in about half an hour. Maybe it would just be nice for him if he saw his father and then...

CLAIRE. No. Why should he be allowed to be here?

PATRICIA. Quite. It's utterly ridiculous.

CAROL. For Andy. He's not seen his father in five years. Who knows when he might see him again.

CLAIRE. So what, just... don't mind us, you do what you want, happy to see you whenever you feel like it, is that it?

CAROL. I'm trying incredibly hard to be rational and grown up about this. Will you please...?

PATRICIA. If you were being rational about this, you'd call the police.

CAROL. What?

PATRICIA. For trespassing.

MARK. Should I go?

CLAIRE. No.

CAROL. Sorry, Mark. I *can* assure you it's not normally like *this*.

CLAIRE. He's not getting his way on this, Mum. This is... I can't believe... If you let him stay I will leave. Why do you even want Andy to see him?

CAROL. This isn't an act of forgiveness. Or generosity. He is here. He has said he wants to see Andy. If that makes Andy happy, then that's all I care about. Today. And if he doesn't show a flicker of recognition then maybe your father might think he needs to do a little more.

CLAIRE. He could hardly do less.

CAROL. Claire. I know.

IAN *re-enters*.

CLAIRE. I'm going for a walk. Mark?

MARK. Yeah, sure.

They leave. A moment.

IAN. Hi, Patricia.

PATRICIA. Ian.

IAN. You look well.

PATRICIA. Oh, please.

A moment.

IAN. I'm sorry for not calling ahead.

PATRICIA. Yes, why was that, Ian?

CAROL. Mum, perhaps you could leave this to us.

PATRICIA. No.

CAROL. No?

PATRICIA. No, I don't trust him. What he might do.

CAROL. We were married for twenty years. If we didn't kill each other then I think we'll make it through the next few minutes.

PATRICIA. Well, where do you want me to go?

CAROL. Is Dad asleep?

PATRICIA. You know your father.

CAROL. Well, can you please go upstairs, just for two minutes?

PATRICIA. Fine. Lovely. So nice to see you, Ian.

PATRICIA *goes upstairs.*

IAN. Well, this is a good start.

A moment.

Not exactly how I imagined it.

CAROL. Sorry to disappoint.

IAN. Can I get a couple of ice cubes?

CAROL. What?

IAN. For the swelling.

He moves toward the kitchen.

CAROL. What are you doing, Ian?

IAN. Pardon?

CAROL. What are you doing here?

IAN. I wanted to see Andy. On his birthday.

CAROL. Why didn't you call?

A moment.

IAN. I didn't think you'd let me come.

CAROL. I'm sorry?

IAN. I presumed I wouldn't have been welcome.

CAROL. But you came anyway.

IAN. Yes.

CAROL. For God's sake… Just get some ice.

IAN goes to the freezer and gets out the ice tray.

IAN. Do you have a tea towel?

CAROL. Third drawer down.

IAN takes out a tea towel, puts some ice in it and holds it to his lip.

IAN. How is he?

CAROL. What?

IAN. Andy?

CAROL. Perhaps you might explain why you're here before we start on the medical review.

IAN. Carol, this wasn't a spur-of-the-moment thing.

CAROL. Well, thanks for letting us know.

A moment.

IAN. It's his twenty-first birthday.

CAROL. I know.

IAN. It was important for me to see him.

CAROL. Really.

IAN. Carol. This isn't totally comfortable for me either.

Silence.

I don't know what to say.

CAROL. Oh, say something, for Christ's sake. If you've been thinking about it so long.

IAN. I can't say everything I need to, can I?

CAROL. Why not?

IAN. Because it would take a while, wouldn't it?

CAROL. It would take until the end of time.

A moment.

IAN. If you honestly can't bear the thought of me seeing him then I'll go.

CAROL. That's right, walk out when things get difficult. That makes a change.

IAN. I have not come here to argue with you. I came here to see Andy. I don't want to start arguing with you again…

CAROL. Oh, thank you, Gandhi.

IAN. But if you can't see a way that that could happen then I will leave.

CAROL. Oh yes, very good. The martyr returns to his wife saying 'I did all I could.'

IAN. Fine, Carol. Will you give him this?

CAROL. You coward. Fucking fight.

A moment.

IAN. What?

CAROL. Fucking fight to see him, you fucking coward.

Silence.

Why do you want to see him, Ian? Why today, why now?

IAN. I've told you. Because it's his birthday.

CAROL. And?

IAN. And what?

CAROL. Why this birthday? What was wrong with the others?

IAN. I am aware I've not been there for him of late…

CAROL. 'Of late'?

IAN.…and that it has been difficult…

CAROL. 'Difficult'?

IAN.…but I want to see my son.

CAROL. So it's the guilt you can't live with, not Andy you can't live without.

IAN. No, it's not just... it's not guilt.

CAROL. And did you honestly expect... did you really think that by coming here... did you actually believe that by just turning up, unannounced, uninvited, with a fucking present, that we would fall to our knees and say 'oh thank you, oh praise the Lord He is risen, alle-fucking-luja'? Did you?

IAN. Of course I...

CAROL. Because actually, Ian, I have done this by myself for the last *twenty* years. Throughout. By myself. You not showing your face for the last five years, it hasn't actually made a blind fucking difference to my life.

Silence.

IAN. And you don't think that might have had anything to do with it?

CAROL. Sorry?

IAN. It doesn't matter.

A moment.

CAROL. No, what do you mean by that?

IAN. It doesn't matter. Please.

Silence.

CAROL. Are you dying?

IAN. Sorry?

CAROL. Well, it's too late for a mid-life crisis, you've done that already. Is it Sylvie? Have you split up with her?

IAN. No.

CAROL. Has she been pressuring you?

IAN. This is nothing to do with Sylvie. Or with Paul.

CAROL. It must be somehow. This *was* your family. They *are* your family. There must be parallels somewhere.

IAN. This isn't fair.

CAROL. They must feel like they're waiting for the axe to fall too, no? If things get a bit tricky. Sorry, how is it not fair?

IAN. You know that's not how things were. Or are.

CAROL. No I don't know, Ian. I don't fucking know at all.

They are silent.

IAN. Life was not easy. Eventually. Between the two of us. Was it?

CAROL. No, it was fucking hard. And for some of us it's got even harder.

IAN. For both of us.

A moment.

CAROL. I honestly can't... I understood when you left us, I understood you couldn't cope. I understood when you met Sylvie, when you had Paul. But not to see him for five years. And then to come here, on his birthday, seeking some sort of absolution from him... that, Ian, I can't even begin to understand.

IAN. I have been in contact with him. I do call him. I write.

CAROL. Yes, he's a voracious reader. And he just loves to chat...

IAN. Fine, I didn't see him because it got too much for me. Is that what you want to hear? I've felt like a cunt for years and now I'm sick of feeling like a cunt.

Silence.

CAROL. Do you want me to applaud your honesty?

IAN. No. I'm just telling you why. It got too...

CAROL. Too much.

Too much what? Too much hassle? Too much like hard work? Too much worry, boredom? Just too much. Too too too fucking much. How can your son be too much?

IAN. It wasn't just my son that was the problem.

CAROL. Sorry?

A moment.

IAN. Carol, it's not going to help us if we rake up the past. It's happened. We're these people now. For better or worse. But you can't stop me seeing my son.

CAROL. If I remember rightly it was you that stopped seeing him.

A moment.

IAN. I think for the first time in my life I'm wishing your mother would come in the room.

CAROL. Don't worry, she'll be listening.

What did you do to your lip anyway?

IAN. I whacked it. On a door.

CAROL. What door?

IAN. Just… the taxi door.

CAROL. When?

IAN. There was a taxi outside when you told me to… and I opened the door too quickly and…

CAROL. You were going to leave?

IAN. You told me to leave.

CAROL. I told you to wait.

IAN. By slamming the door in my face.

CAROL. Well, wow, Ian. What terrifying perseverance.

IAN. I came back.

CAROL. Really? What for? A plaster?

Silence.

What's he like when you call him?

IAN. What do you mean?

CAROL. Does he laugh? Does it sound like he recognises your voice?

IAN. Yes… the little gurgle.

CAROL. That's not a laugh.

IAN. I know what his laugh sounds like.

CAROL. But not what it looks like.

IAN. He's not a stranger to me, Carol. I was pretty good for the first ten years…

CAROL. 'Pretty good'! What do you mean by 'pretty good'?

IAN. You did not have to do it all alone.

CAROL. When he was ill, who did they call? When he had a wheelchair fitting, who went? Who stayed awake in hospital chairs night after night making sure his fucking oxygen mask didn't slip off his face, Ian?… Ian?

IAN. You. And you never wanted it any other way.

CAROL's *mobile rings. They stare at each other. Eventually she checks it.*

CAROL. It's Andy's carer. Do you want to answer it?

IAN. Do you think I…?

CAROL. I'm being sarcastic.

She answers it.

Yes, Murat?… right has he had the Ventolin?… Why not?… Do it now, make sure he gets all of it, okay?… Call me in ten minutes, tell me if he's any better… okay, bye.

IAN. Is he alright?

CAROL. He's been wheezy the last couple of days. I'll see how he is when he gets here. It is his birthday after all, it's the least we could expect.

IAN. Do you not think you should call a doctor now? Let him know.

CAROL. Is this advice?

IAN. Oh, for fuck's *sake.*

CAROL. Sorry?

IAN. Do you not see? It's exactly this… Can't you fucking see?

CAROL. What?

IAN. What was the point in me sticking around, Carol? What was the point trying to have a relationship with him? You wouldn't let me. You didn't care what I thought. Me or Claire. You weren't interested in being a family. All you cared about was him. Well guess what, I cared too. But I wanted to be a family.

Silence.

MARK *and* CLAIRE *enter.*

CLAIRE. Why's he still here?

IAN. Look, I realise I should have phoned ahead. But I want to see Andy on his birthday. And I'd love to see you too.

CLAIRE. I'm going upstairs. Let me know when he's gone.

CLAIRE *goes upstairs.*

MARK. I'm Mark, by the way.

IAN. Hi, I'm…

CLAIRE (*off*). Grandma, what are you…?

PATRICIA (*off*). I was just coming down the stairs.

MARK *passes* PATRICIA *as she enters and he goes upstairs.*

I think it's better if I say this now rather than risk it coming out wrong in the heat of the moment: I find it very difficult to even look at you. What you have put my family through in the last fifteen years I would not wish on my worst enemy. Which, unsurprisingly, is you. You are a hateful, hateful, loathsome man. I have imagined you in countless accidents over the years, not all of which have been fatal, but none of them have captured satisfactorily the ferocity of my antipathy towards you. It burns inside of me. And if you can imagine that fire, the strength with which that blazes, it is like a match compared to the furnace that rages within your daughter.

A moment.

IAN. Thank you for your dispassionate analysis.

PATRICIA. Right, I have said what I wanted to say. Now, if you are staying, perhaps you'll clean up the mud your shoes brought in on your way to the bathroom. There are J-cloths by the sink.

IAN goes to the sink, PATRICIA *sits.*

Darling, perhaps the lasagne should be taken out, if there are to be delays. I imagine Claire won't want to eat until after our guest has gone.

CAROL *takes the lasagne out.*

IAN. I do also want to see...

PATRICIA. And when you've finished with the floor there is one elderly lady here who, much against the advice of her doctor, will probably expire if she doesn't have a gin and tonic.

IAN. Certainly.

PATRICIA. When you've finished the floor.

Silence.

PATRICIA *watches as* IAN *gets down on his hands and knees and begins scrubbing the carpet.*

A long silence. Very long.

CAROL. Is Dad okay, does he need waking?

PATRICIA. I don't think we need subject him to this, do you, darling?

A moment.

CAROL. I'm going to check on Claire.

CAROL *goes to the stairs.*

(*To* IAN.) See if she'll come down.

She exits upstairs.

IAN *finishes cleaning the floor and returns to the sink.*

IAN. The floor's done.

PATRICIA. Three ice cubes and a slice of lemon.

IAN. I'll make it a strong one.

PATRICIA. I'll do the jokes.

   IAN *begins to make the gin and tonic*.

IAN. Have you been keeping well?

PATRICIA. I'm afraid I have, yes.

   A moment.

IAN. Sorry, do you know where the lemons are?

   Silence.

   Patricia, the lemons?

   Silence.

   I see your hearing's deteri / orated.

PATRICIA. / Where they've always been.

IAN. I do understand I'm not your favourite person in the world, Patricia. I don't expect you to forgive me. I'm here because I want to try and have a relationship with my son and my daughter, okay?

   Can you understand that?

   A moment.

PATRICIA. And you think it's going to be as easy as that, do you?

IAN. No, it won't be easy, but I can try.

PATRICIA. I see.

IAN. People can change, Patricia.

PATRICIA. Evidently.

IAN. I know you all feel I've let you down. But Carol needs help. And I want to help her.

PATRICIA. She won't let you help her, Ian.

IAN. Well, I want to try to make sure she will.

PATRICIA. She doesn't want to be helped.

A moment.

IAN. And why do you think that is?

PATRICIA. Do you really need me to explain?

A moment.

Do you remember when Claire was born?

IAN. How do you mean?

PATRICIA. Which bit don't you understand? Claire, your
daughter?

IAN. Yes, of course I remember when she was born.

PATRICIA. Do you remember that feeling, this perfect, helpless
person you'd created, entirely dependent on you?

A moment.

Sorry, I'm presuming you felt something.

IAN. Yes, I remember.

PATRICIA. Well, that feeling... that has lasted a lifetime for
Carol. For Andy. That's a terribly powerful emotion to
sustain for twenty-one years. And you could have shared that
feeling but you left. You left and Claire grew up and now...
he is everything. That's your legacy. A quite unimpeachable
love. And she is not going to let you spoil that for her.

IAN hands PATRICIA her gin and tonic.

IAN. No. She never did.

PATRICIA. Well, it is now killing her.

A moment.

IAN. What?

PATRICIA (*drinks to embolden herself*). It'll be very sad, of
course, but Andrew is going to die. Obviously we all are, but
Andrew is expected to die, sooner than most. And
furthermore, and forgive me for saying this, I hope he is
going to die. I love him more than I ever thought I would.

He's taught me more about life and its ridiculousness than anyone or anything else. But I hope he will die. I hope he will die so that Carol can live.

There will be no guilt for her. She has been an exceptional mother, far better a parent than I ever was, far better obviously than you will ever be. She has done everything she could have.

But she will not let it happen. And it is now killing her. Because the kind of love that Carol has for Andy... it can destroy you.

Silence.

IAN. I know.

PATRICIA. And yet you chose to do nothing about it.

IAN. Yes.

PATRICIA. Might I ask why?

A moment.

IAN. Because I had started to hope he might die too.

A moment.

PATRICIA. So why the change of heart?

Silence.

IAN. I don't know... It's not easy feeling like an arsehole all the time.

CLAIRE *and* MARK *come down, followed by* CAROL.

CLAIRE. You can stay until Andy gets here and then you can take him for a walk and then you can go.

IAN. Claire, please don't...

CLAIRE. It's that or nothing.

CAROL. / Claire, just...

IAN. / I'd love to be able to...

CLAIRE. No, I'm saying if he wants to see Andy he can see him and then he can go.

Well?

IAN. Do I have a choice?

CLAIRE. Did we have one?

A moment.

IAN. Alright, fine, yes. Thank you.

CLAIRE *sits and pointedly picks up a magazine and begins to read.*

Hi, I'm Ian, by the way.

MARK. Yeah, yeah. Mark.

IAN. Hi, Mark.

A moment.

CAROL. Mark, can I get you anything [to drink]…?

MARK. A beer would be great, please.

CAROL *goes to the fridge.*

CAROL. Ian?

CLAIRE. He can get it himself.

IAN *makes to get up.*

CAROL. I think I can manage.

IAN. Thank you.

CAROL *opens two cans of beer and begins to pour them into pint glasses.*

Silence.

PATRICIA. Mark is a poet, that's right, isn't it?

MARK. Yeah, yeah, that's right.

IAN. Oh right. Great.

MARK. Performance poet.

IAN. Really? Great. Where do you do that?

MARK. Oh, all over. Just, you know, pubs and bars and...

CLAIRE. Glastonbury.

MARK. Yeah, yeah, did that... last year.

IAN. Glastonbury? That must have been fun.

MARK. Yeah, I was quite early on so... not a big crowd but yeah, yeah... it was fun.

A moment.

IAN. I've never been.

MARK. Well, it's not going anywhere, still time. Most of the bands playing these days are your generation anyway. I mean... I mean they're all...

IAN. Old gits?

MARK. I should learn to shut up, shouldn't I?

IAN (*laughs*). You're alright.

Silence.

PATRICIA. Why do people want to hear them?

CLAIRE. Grandma.

PATRICIA. I mean, rather than read them, why do they want to hear them?

MARK. Good question... erm, I can't really answer for them to be honest. I guess for me some of the poems I write, I write to be heard and some of them I write to be read. There's a difference in the language and the structure. And the experience, I guess. For them, maybe. Sharing in something. Together. Reacting differently, but having the same experience.

PATRICIA. Oh. How fascinating.

Silence.

IAN. Claire shown you any of hers?

MARK. Sorry?

IAN. From when she was little.

MARK. What?

IAN. She used to write. Poems. Little...

CLAIRE. No I didn't.

IAN. Yes you did. 'The Peculiar Mongoose'?

CAROL. Oh yes, Mark, that was a good one.

She brings the beers over to MARK *and* IAN.

IAN (*to* CAROL). Thanks.

MARK. You never said you...

CLAIRE. It wasn't a poem.

IAN. It rhymed, didn't it?

MARK. That's a start.

IAN. There you go.

CLAIRE. It was a song.

MARK. I look forward to hearing it.

CLAIRE. Yeah right.

IAN. You've got a treat in store.

CLAIRE. Just stop it.

IAN. What?

A moment.

CLAIRE. Do you think I'm going to say 'Oh yes, oh the fun we had?'

A moment.

IAN. I was just remembering...

CLAIRE. Well don't. Because I don't remember. I don't remember the good times, I don't remember you at all. If I do, I stop remembering.

Silence.

MARK. Carol, do you / need a hand?

IAN. / And does that help?

CLAIRE. Sorry?

CAROL. I'm alright thanks.

IAN. Does it help? To obliterate me like that.

CLAIRE. Help? Yes it helps, why do you care?

IAN. Because you're my daughter.

CLAIRE (*suddenly, shouting*). Don't call me that!

CAROL. Claire!

IAN. Why, you want me to say you're not?

CLAIRE. I don't call you my father.

IAN. Well, sorry, I'm not going to return the compliment.

CLAIRE. Why not?

IAN. Because you're my daughter, I'm proud of that, / I'm not going to deny it.

CLAIRE. / Yes, you must have been so proud.

Really? You did.

IAN. I did not stop wanting to be your father.

CLAIRE. Just not Andy's. Sorry, you don't get to choose.

IAN. It wasn't a choice. Do you think if I had thought you and I would…

CLAIRE. What did you suppose was going to happen?

A moment.

IAN. I'm sorry, my crystal ball must have been a bit fuzzy.

CLAIRE. Was it the same one that told you it was a good idea to come today?

A moment.

CAROL. Well, Mark, you think you've had fun so far, just wait until Andy gets here.

IAN. Please don't…

CLAIRE. Don't what?

IAN. Claire. I brought you up for nearly twenty years…

CLAIRE. Seventeen.

IAN.…just, please…

CLAIRE. 'Please'?

A moment.

My God, do you not understand? Are you really that…? If we were happy, if we were a family then what you did… do you not see… what you did makes not being there…

IAN. I know. I know that, Claire. I know you must have felt rejected. But it's you that's rejected me since.

CAROL. Ian…

CLAIRE. Fucking… Why do you think that is?

IAN. Because you're angry with me I know, but…

CLAIRE. Don't flatter yourself, I've not had time to be angry with you.

IAN. I know that's not true.

CLAIRE. It is true. I'm sorry, I've been busy.

IAN. Busy?

CLAIRE. Someone had to look after Andy.

CAROL. Claire, / come on…

IAN. / That's ridiculous.

CLAIRE. What? I had to become a mum overnight.

IAN. Don't exaggerate.

CLAIRE. I'm not!

IAN. Then why are you behaving like a child.

A moment.

CLAIRE. Get the fuck out.

IAN. You don't know what you'd do, Claire.

CLAIRE. I said, get the fuck…

CAROL. Claire, calm down.

IAN. You keeping on hating me won't make me think I was wrong.

A moment.

I'm not your mother. I couldn't do what she does. / I'm different. Worse, if you want, but different. I don't mind her judging me but not you.

CAROL. / Ian…

CLAIRE. What's that supposed to mean?

IAN. It's hard being a parent. You don't…

CLAIRE. Don't you dare patronise me.

IAN. You can't understand… It was fucking difficult. Andy was fucking difficult, you were fucking difficult…

CLAIRE. And didn't we know it.

IAN. You knew we loved you.

CLAIRE. And then you left.

IAN. And if I hadn't it might have been even worse.

CLAIRE. How convenient.

IAN. Oh, for fuck's sake, Claire…

CAROL. Ian…

IAN. No, I'm sorry, she can't… She has never stopped to try and understand. What we went through…

CAROL. Don't bring me into this.

IAN. Never, no, Carol, never just thought… just thought what it might actually mean to be an adult.

Silence.

CLAIRE. No, I don't know what it's like to be an adult, that's right, or what it's like to be a parent.

But I will.

IAN. Yes, and you'll be a great mother, I'm sure, and you'll never make any mistakes.

CLAIRE. No, I'm going to know.

A moment.

CAROL. What?

MARK. Claire, don't…

CLAIRE. I'm going to know what it's like.

A moment.

Okay?

Silence.

BRIAN (*off*). Could I possibly have a lift up?

Silence.

CAROL. Ian… Mark, would you mind?

MARK. Sure… I'll…

MARK *goes to leave.*

CAROL. Ian?

IAN (*to* CLAIRE). Are you serious?

CAROL. Ian, will you help lift?

A moment.

IAN. Are you serious? You're…?

CAROL. Ian, now! Mum?

IAN *and* MARK *go towards Andy's bedroom.*

PATRICIA. I'll just… I'll be upstairs.

PATRICIA *heads up the stairs.*

CLAIRE *and* CAROL *are alone.*

CAROL. Is that true?

CLAIRE.…

CAROL. Claire, tell me now. Is that true?

CLAIRE. What?

CAROL. Is it true that you're pregnant?

CLAIRE. That's usually how you get to be a parent.

CAROL. I'm sorry?

CLAIRE. Yes, I'm pregnant.

Silence.

I was going to tell you this evening. That's why I didn't want him here.

CAROL. It's his grandchild too.

CLAIRE. Fine.

A moment.

CAROL. How long?

CLAIRE. Only three months.

CAROL. Three months?

CLAIRE. Three and a half.

Silence.

CAROL. Why didn't you tell me before?

CLAIRE. You're not supposed to tell anyone until three months.

CAROL. For God's sake.

CLAIRE. What?

CAROL. You could have told me if you wanted to. It's not a law.

CLAIRE. Well… there you go.

CAROL. Rather do it like this then, yes?

CLAIRE. It's my life.

CAROL. It is not just your life, Claire. You are part of a *family*.

CLAIRE *puts her head in her hands*.

Don't try to make me feel bad.

CLAIRE. I'm not trying to do anything.

A moment.

CAROL. So, what, do you not want it?

CLAIRE. No. I mean, no, I'm happy.

CAROL. You look it.

A moment.

What were you thinking?

CLAIRE. What?

CAROL. Why didn't you tell me?

CLAIRE. Who knows.

CAROL. You must have been thinking something, Claire, for fuck's sake.

A moment.

How long have you known him?

CLAIRE. Years. But we've only… we've only been together about a year.

CAROL. A year.

A moment.

Have you met his parents?

CLAIRE. His dad, yes. His mum's dead.

A moment.

CAROL. And does he know?

CLAIRE. Why does that matter?

CAROL. It matters.

CLAIRE. I don't think so.

Silence.

CAROL. Well, this is just how I dreamed it would happen.

CLAIRE. I haven't done this to annoy you.

CAROL. You haven't annoyed me, Claire. I'm not *annoyed*.

CLAIRE. Don't… This is mine, okay? I had to decide what I wanted to do. I didn't need you to decide for me.

CAROL. Decide for you? Why would I decide for you?

A moment.

What do you mean, you didn't need me to decide for you?

CLAIRE. It doesn't matter. I'm telling you now okay? / Mark and I are having a baby. Maybe you could be pleased for us. //

CAROL. / What is that supposed to mean?

// Pleased for you? Yes, if you had treated me like you cared what I thought, maybe I would be. Obviously you don't, though, / so why does it matter.

CLAIRE. / Don't make this about yourself.

CAROL. I'm sorry?

CLAIRE. Just for once, let me be happy.

Silence.

CAROL. 'Just for once let'…?

CLAIRE. That's…

CAROL. 'For once'?

A moment.

Good luck as a mother, Claire. You're going to need it. Children can be horribly ungrateful cunts.

CLAIRE. 'Ungrateful'? Don't you dare…

CAROL. What?

CLAIRE. I have fucking… Don't call me ungrateful. You're fucking lucky to have had me.

CAROL. Am I, Claire? Am I? I've been so lucky, haven't I, so blessed. A son with a mental age of ten months / and a daughter with an emotional one of a nine-year-old. Oh, is it mine?

CLAIRE. / That's not my fault.

CLAIRE. What?

CAROL. Is it my fault, is that what you're saying? My *fault* Andy was born the way he is, is that it? / Or is it my fault you could never speak up for yourself? //

CLAIRE. / Don't be ridiculous.

// How could I with you around?

CAROL. And why do you think it is I've had to shout so loud, Claire? Because otherwise no one would ever fucking listen to me.

Silence.

You think you became a mum overnight when your father left, you've no idea… Do you know what it's like. / Every time a phone rings, no you're not aware, Claire, every time someone drops round to say hello, every text I get he's died. In my mind he's died, okay? Every time he coughs I'm imagining what to say at his funeral. That's my life, Claire. It's fucking endless. Do you understand that? For some of us it's not been a choice. It's not made us feel good about ourselves. We've just had to do it, because no one else will. Just had to watch ourselves rot. You think you know what that's like? // Do you?

CLAIRE. / We're all well aware.

// Yes I do, / some of us have been here too.

CAROL. / No, Claire, you don't because otherwise you wouldn't do what you have just done.

CLAIRE. Fine, it was awful, it was devastating, what do you want me to say?

CAROL. Thank you, Mum, thanks for making sure I was okay. And well done. Thanks for not putting a pillow over his head. Thank you for going into the toilet to cry. Thank you for still trying to be a person. And guess what, I'm pregnant and happy and here's your grandchild, look how normal and boring and content he is. That's all I've ever wanted and you couldn't even do that for me. How does that make me feel? Hmm? I'll tell you how. Why am I even here? Why don't I just take Andy and fuck off out of everybody's lives? Because we are obviously in the way of people enjoying themselves.

A moment.

So I'm sorry you think I've never let you be happy. I'm sorry you can't share your life with any of us. But I can assure you, it is a fucking lonely way to exist.

Silence.

CLAIRE. I've not said it's not been difficult. I'm not saying you haven't done everything you could. For me and for Andy. Don't twist this out of proportion...

CAROL. 'Out of proportion', Claire, you've...

CLAIRE. I didn't tell you because I am scared. The world scares me. Okay? Because of what's happened. And I don't know what to do about that.

CAROL. Be brave.

A moment.

CLAIRE. That's not enough.

CAROL. Well, I'm sorry. It's all there is.

CLAIRE *begins to cry. A while before* CAROL *speaks.*

Do you love him?

CLAIRE. I can't... I can't be let down again.

CAROL. Do you love him?

CLAIRE. I just want to be sure.

CAROL. You can't be. I was sure.

A moment.

Would you be happier if you didn't have it?

CLAIRE. What?

CAROL. At least be brave enough to answer that.

A moment.

CLAIRE. Would you have been?

Silence.

The bedroom door opens and IAN *puts his head out.*

IAN. Can I...?

CAROL. What / is it?

CLAIRE. / Get out!

CAROL. What is it, Ian?

IAN. Look... I wanted to say...

CLAIRE. Will you get out!

IAN. I just want to say I'm sorry for upsetting you. I was out
of order.

CLAIRE. Get out!

IAN. No, just this and then I'll go if you want. I'm sure this
isn't how you imagined telling everyone and that was my
fault and I'm sorry. Alright? I'm sorry. I didn't realise.
Obviously. But I'm thrilled for...

CLAIRE. Don't...

IAN. Okay. Fine. I just wanted to say, congratulations. And sorry.

A moment.

CLAIRE. Don't you ever get bored of apologising?

IAN. Yes.

But some things worth doing *are* boring.

A moment.

CAROL. Did you write that down beforehand?

IAN. No, Carol.

A moment.

But I'm quite pleased with it.

CAROL. We can tell.

MARK, IAN *and* BRIAN *enter.*

BRIAN (*singing*). 'If I knew you were pregnant, I'd have baked a cake… baked a cake… baked a cake.'

CLAIRE. / Granddad, don't…

CAROL. / Dad. Can you just…

BRIAN. Fantastic news. I am so pleased for you both.

CAROL. Dad, don't…

MARK. Sorry, I thought I better… explain.

BRIAN. Carol, does this not call for some kind of bubbles?

CLAIRE. Oh / no, don't…

CAROL. / No, Dad, it's not…

BRIAN. Come on, it's a double celebration now.

A moment.

CAROL. I'll have a look.

CLAIRE. Don't. You don't have to…

CAROL. Well… don't get your hopes up.

CAROL *moves to the kitchen, as* PATRICIA *comes down the stairs and goes to* CAROL, MARK *goes to* CLAIRE *and* IAN *helps* BRIAN *into a chair.*

MARK. Okay?

IAN. Alright, Brian, let's sit you down.

CLAIRE. Yeah, yeah. Fine.

CAROL. Hear everything, did you?

PATRICIA. I didn't even have to strain.

BRIAN. You see, I don't need the one… two… three.

CAROL. Mark, can I say…

CLAIRE. Mum, don't…

PATRICIA. Carol…

CAROL. No, I'd like to… I'm sorry. I can't say I'm not surprised. I can't say I'm not hurt.

PATRICIA. Carol, not…

CAROL. He might as well know now, Mum. This isn't a mother's dream, I'm sure you'll understand, I'm sure you're probably a little embarrassed yourself.

A moment.

All I *can* say is… is that as an introduction to the family… I wish it wasn't quite so representative.

A moment.

CLAIRE (*laughs nervously*). Mum!

BRIAN. She's right, Mark. A day like this? If I had a penny…

MARK. Still got time to make a run for it, have I?

PATRICIA (*at* IAN). I wouldn't.

CAROL *opens the fridge.*

CAROL. Right, if Dad insists, bubbles…

BRIAN. Yes!

CAROL. Is Fanta any good?

BRIAN. No!

MARK (*laughs*). What year?

CLAIRE. There might be one… check in the cupboard there.

MARK. Where?

CLAIRE. / Just…

IAN. / Just… it's alright, I'll go.

MARK. Where are your glasses kept?

CLAIRE. I'll get them.

MARK. You sit there. Get used to it.

CLAIRE. I'm not an invalid.

BRIAN. Don't knock it till you try it.

IAN *pulls out a bottle of cheap fizz from the cupboard.*

IAN. Er, it's not champagne and it's not cold but…

MARK. You can taste it better when it's warm.

IAN. I could go to the shop…?

CAROL. No. That'll do. Give it here, I'll put it in the freezer for a minute.

As IAN *opens the bottle.*

IAN. Sorry, I've er… too late.

MARK. How many of us are there?

CAROL. Er, one, two, three… Mum?

PATRICIA. Just wet the bottom of the glass.

BRIAN. Yes, and drench the sides.

IAN. Brian, do you want…?

BRIAN. God yes.

MARK. Good man.

BRIAN. Should somebody make a toast?

MARK. Why not?

BRIAN. Anyone?

CAROL. Ian?

A moment.

IAN. Me?

MARK. Alright then.

IAN. No, I meant…

CAROL. Go on, we're all ears.

A moment.

What, you've not written anything?

IAN. Erm…

BRIAN. I can do it.

CLAIRE. No.

CAROL. It's alright, Dad. I'm sure Ian has something to say.

A moment.

IAN. Well… Thank you, Carol, Claire… Right, well I'd like to say… well, as Brian said we've got a couple of things to celebrate today. Firstly, Andy's birthday… but, er… I guess we'll save that toast till he's here… But also, I'd like to make a toast to my daughter. And her boyfriend, her partner, her… her…

MARK. Mark's fine.

IAN. To Mark, yes. And their baby. Their baby. May he be healthy… may he or she be… happy… and loved. To Claire and Mark.

BRIAN. To Claire and Mark.

Silence.

PATRICIA. Excuse me, does this mean I am to be a great-grandmother because I'm not sure I like that at all.

CAROL. Mother, what a legacy. 'Loving wife, sister, mother, grandmother, great-grandmother' – we'll never fit it all on the headstone.

PATRICIA. Then I imagine you'll have to omit the 'loving'.

BRIAN. A baby. This poor family. Just what we need, someone else who needs a hand taking a crap.

CLAIRE. Granddad!

CAROL. At least he'll be in experienced hands.

PATRICIA. Is this something you'd write about, then, Mark?

MARK. Sorry?

PATRICIA. I imagine impending fatherhood must stir the muse.

MARK. Er, yeah, yeah… I guess.

PATRICIA. May we hear?

CLAIRE. Grandma!

PATRICIA. I thought you said he performed for strangers. I know we are imminently family but we are essentially still strangers.

CLAIRE. He's not the entertainment.

PATRICIA. I thought it might be nice, I'm sorry.

CLAIRE. Do you want him to put a flat cap down for some pennies as well?

PATRICIA. If that's all you think he's worth.

MARK. You want to hear a poem of mine, is that what you're getting at, Patricia?

PATRICIA. Surely you've something celebratory for an occasion like this?

A moment.

MARK. Okay.

CLAIRE. Don't, you don't have to.

MARK. No, it's okay. Okay, I er… I wrote this when Claire told me she was pregnant. But I've not said it out loud because, well, we, er… well, I haven't.

PATRICIA. A premiere, how exciting.

CAROL. Shall we gather round?

MARK. No, it's alright, you don't have to…

CAROL. Come on, everyone round the table.

CLAIRE. Mum, he said…

MARK. It's fine, it's fine.

They all gather to the sitting-room area.

BRIAN. It's like the *Canterbury Tales*.

MARK. Right. Er… it's too late to back out now, isn't it?

BRIAN. 'Fraid so, kid.

MARK. My big mouth. Right, er… it's called 'Three O'Clock':

A moment.

PATRICIA. Is it long?

CLAIRE. Grandma!

PATRICIA. I'm just wondering if I should sit down…

MARK. It's not long *and* it rhymes.

PATRICIA. Perfect.

A moment.

MARK.
> 'Oh crap, what's that?'
> 'What d'you think?' 'Is it me?'
> 'Sure is, what's the time?'
> 'I don't know, I can't see.
>
> 'Are you sure it's my turn?'
> 'Don't you dare, up you get'
> 'But the landing's so cold'
> 'And his nappy's so wet.'
>
> 'If you just do this one
> I'll do the next four.'
> 'Except I did the last one
> And the last two before.'
>
> 'Alright, fifty quid
> And I'll clean the loos.'
> 'Do you really think that's
> Going to better this snooze?'
>
> 'I think he's quietening down,
> Can you hear, not a peep…
> Oh man, how'd we get one
> Allergic to sleep.'

But for you and for it
I'd not sleep a wink.
I'd just stare at its face
And at yours and I'd think

How did I have such luck
And what did I do so right.
To get a woman and child
I'd never stop holding tight.

That's it.

They all warmly applaud.

CAROL. That's lovely, Mark.

BRIAN. Bravo, sir, bravo.

CLAIRE (*awkwardly*). Thank you.

BRIAN. You're a smooth operator, aren't you?

MARK. I don't know about that.

A moment.

Right, well, I need a drink. Who's for more warm bubbles?

PATRICIA. And what was it you said you did apart from the poetry?

CAROL. / Mum!

CLAIRE. / Grandma!

MARK. I'm, er… I'm a trained carpenter as well.

PATRICIA. Oh good.

MARK. Is it?

PATRICIA. Just… I mean, to support the baby.

BRIAN. If it was good enough for Jesus, Mark, it's just about good enough for Patricia.

CAROL's phone rings.

CAROL. I am not interrupting the party. I am taking it in here. Everybody carry on.

CAROL *goes into Andy's room.*

MARK. What's your party piece then, Patricia?

BRIAN. She can keep her mouth shut for up to twenty-five seconds.

PATRICIA. Brian!

MARK. This I have to see.

CLAIRE. Yeah right. Even when we'd play sleeping lions she was allowed to sleep-talk.

PATRICIA. Is this bullying? I think this is coming dangerously close to bullying.

IAN. Sleeping dragons, didn't we call it?

A moment.

PATRICIA. Ian, flames cannot be fanned by a broken bellows.

Silence, then bemused laughter from all except IAN.

MARK. Now *that's* poetry.

BRIAN. And she doesn't even have to think. Stick around long enough, Mark, you'd fill a book.

MARK. Won't you share the embarrassment, Brian? Any special skills?

CLAIRE. He doesn't need encouraging.

MARK. Oh really?

BRIAN. Spoons, please!

PATRICIA. Now you've done it.

BRIAN. I said, spoons!

CLAIRE *goes to the kitchen and gets a pair of dessert spoons from a drawer.*

CLAIRE. You'll remember this, Mark, your first time hearing Brian Wilkinson's spoons.

MARK. It's an honour.

PATRICIA. But almost certainly not your last.

BRIAN. Today, ladies and gentlemen, in honour of our esteemed guest, I'd like to play my spoons as a prelude, an hors d'oeuvre if you will, to some lines from a little poet from the countryside.

She passes BRIAN *the spoons.*

CLAIRE. He's going off-road.

BRIAN. Ian?

IAN *helps* BRIAN *to his feet.*

PATRICIA. He's got someone to show off to.

BRIAN. Someone Mark here could teach a thing or two about comprehensibility. His name is William and I performed these lines, without accompaniment, to a class full of beautiful women only last month. Pray silence for a spoon-roll please.

He wildly plays a spoon solo before stopping and taking in his audience.

'The quality of mercy is not strained.
It droppeth as the gentle…'

PATRICIA. You said you were studying *Love's Labour's Lost*.

BRIAN. That's this month. *Merchant of Venice* was last month.

'It droppeth as the gentle rain from heaven
Upon the place beneath…'

PATRICIA. The only man in the class and they cast you in a woman's part.

BRIAN. How'd you know it was a woman's part?

PATRICIA. It's very famous, Brian.

BRIAN. Is it? Oh. Well, just listen.

'It is twice blest:
It blesseth him that gives and him that takes.
'Tis mightiest in the mightiest.'

Patricia, I can hear you laughing. I can't do it if you're laughing.

PATRICIA. Who in God's name plays the men?

BRIAN. She's called Wendy.

PATRICIA. Poor Wendy.

BRIAN. You're telling me. Voice deeper than a bullfrog and a moustache like Windsor Davies.

PATRICIA. I'd have thought you'd have been a perfect Richard III.

BRIAN. Oh charming. Lovely. Fine, I shall take my gifts elsewhere. Your loss, your loss the lot of you.

PATRICIA. I think we'll survive.

MARK. Who's next, then? Ian? What you bringing to the party?

IAN. Oh no. You're alright.

MARK. Come on.

IAN. No, really. I'm not much of a performer.

MARK. Ah, spoilsport. Claire? Hidden talents?

CLAIRE. If I had any I wouldn't hide them.

MARK. Don't give me that. What about these songs?

CLAIRE. Like I can remember them.

MARK. Come on, don't just let Brian and I be the show-offs.

CLAIRE. Really, no.

MARK. If I begged?

CLAIRE. Begged?

MARK. Really begged.

CLAIRE. Tempting, but no.

MARK. You know I'm not above begging, don't you?

BRIAN (*raising his spoons*). I can accompany you.

CLAIRE. I don't want to.

IAN. I'll sing it with you.

A moment.

CLAIRE. What?

IAN. 'What a Peculiar Mongoose.' I'll sing it with you.

A moment.

CLAIRE. Go on then.

IAN. Really?

A moment.

After three?

CLAIRE. Go on.

A moment.

IAN. One. Two. Three.

A moment.

> What a peculiar mongoose,
> Walking down the stairs.
> What a peculiar mongoose,
> No troubles or no cares.

He waits. So does CLAIRE.

> He puts on his hat, he puts on his shoes,
> He picks up his bag, no time to lose.

He waits.

> This very peculiar mongoose.

CAROL *enters quickly from Andy's room with his pillow. Through the next she continues to get other things for him from the kitchen.*

CAROL. Claire, can you make me up a bag?

CLAIRE. What? No.

CAROL. Yep.

BRIAN. Oh no, Carol.

IAN. What's up?

CAROL. What do you think?

IAN. What?

CLAIRE. / How many nights?

BRIAN. / Oh dear.

CAROL. A couple, to start with.

PATRICIA. Oh, Carol.

IAN. What's wrong?

CLAIRE *goes upstairs*.

CAROL. He's got worse. The nebuliser hasn't seemed to do anything. They're going to take him straight to the hospital.

IAN. Can't he come here first?

CAROL. No, he can't.

IAN. I thought you said…

CAROL. Things change quickly, Ian.

BRIAN. Not too bad, though, is he?

CAROL. We'll see.

MARK. Can I do anything?

CAROL. See if Claire wants a hand.

MARK. Sure.

MARK *goes upstairs*.

IAN. Is it an infection?

CAROL. Probably.

PATRICIA. Are you going to drive?

CAROL. Er, yes… Claire'll have to come with me I guess… the parking…

PATRICIA. Well, I'm coming with you too.

CAROL. No, it's alright. You don't have to all…

PATRICIA. I want to see my grandson on his birthday, Carol. If that's in a hospital, so be it. He should be with his family.

CAROL. Okay. Thank you.

PATRICIA *goes to get her coat.*

IAN. Can I come?

A moment.

CAROL. No.

A moment.

IAN. I'd like to.

CAROL. No. I don't [want you to]… Stay here.

IAN. I'd prefer to…

CAROL. Stay here. Look after Dad.

BRIAN. I don't need looking after.

IAN. Are you sure?

CAROL. Yes. I'm sure.

IAN. Okay… okay, if that's what you want.

CAROL. None of this is what I want, Ian.

CLAIRE *and* MARK *descend the stairs.*

CLAIRE. Here are your things. Does Andy need anything?

CAROL. Er, I think they've got everything. Maybe just put a pair of pyjamas in a plastic bag. They're on the middle shelf…

CLAIRE. Okay.

CLAIRE *goes into Andy's room.*

MARK. I'm really sorry, Carol. On his birthday, it's such a shame.

CAROL. We've learnt not to be too precious about special occasions. I think this is the third birthday we've spent in hospital. Never admitted on the actual day before though, that's a novelty at least.

MARK. How long does he tend to stay in?

CAROL. It depends. It's been days, it's been weeks. Five weeks was the worst. For a chest infection. First few days are the most important though.

MARK. Christ, poor feller.

CAROL. Yeah, poor feller.

A moment.

MARK. Look, I'm sorry if… We should have…

CAROL. Don't worry. It wasn't your fault.

Silence.

MARK. Have you far to go?

CAROL. No, it's only five minutes in the car – one bright spot at least. One reason why I've never moved.

PATRICIA (*to* BRIAN). You'll be okay?

BRIAN. For about three days. Then I might need a hand.

PATRICIA. Right, I'm ready.

CAROL. Well then, if *you're* ready…

IAN. Will you call me and let me know how he is? Maybe I can come tomorrow.

CAROL. I don't have your number.

IAN. Claire does.

CAROL. I don't think she does.

IAN. She does. I gave it to her.

CAROL. I don't think she does.

A moment.

IAN. I'll text it her again.

CAROL. Fine. Bye, Dad.

BRIAN. Give him a kiss from me.

CAROL. Yep.

PATRICIA. Be good.

BRIAN. I'll try.

As PATRICIA *and* CAROL *leave…*

PATRICIA. Wait, the nutritionist. Should we call her and tell her not to come?

CAROL. Nope. Fuck her. Let her be disappointed too.

CAROL *closes the door behind them.*

CLAIRE *re-enters.*

CLAIRE. I put some bibs in… Have they gone?

IAN. They're just outside.

CLAIRE. Right.

MARK. I don't mind coming, you know. I'd like to.

CLAIRE. It's fine. I don't want you meeting him in hospital.

MARK. You know it wouldn't bother me.

CLAIRE. I know, it would me though. Sorry.

MARK. Call me when you get there then, okay?

CLAIRE. Yeah. Do you know what time the trains are?

MARK. It's fine, I'll phone.

CLAIRE. What are you going to do?

IAN. I'm, er… I'm going to head off. Your mum doesn't… I'll come tomorrow.

CLAIRE. Sure.

IAN. I'll call you / later though.

CLAIRE. / Granddad, are you going to be okay?

BRIAN. Don't worry about me.

CLAIRE. I'll ring to let you know everything's alright.

BRIAN. I'm not so good getting to the phone, love.

CLAIRE. Er... well, I'll call and if everything's okay I'll hang up after four rings.

BRIAN. Gotcha.

CLAIRE. Okay? Four rings, everything's fine.

BRIAN. Understood.

CLAIRE. Call you later.

BRIAN. Ta-ta, love.

CLAIRE. Bye.

MARK. Bye. Hope everything's alright.

CLAIRE and MARK kiss.

I'm so excited, by the way.

CLAIRE. Me too.

They kiss again.

MARK. I love you.

CLAIRE. Yeah.

I am too.

A car horn is heard.

Speak later.

They kiss again.

IAN. Bye.

CLAIRE leaves.

Silence.

BRIAN. Same time next year, everyone?

MARK. Bit of singing, bit of champagne, been to worse.

BRIAN. You poor thing. Oh, poor Carol.

MARK. She seems a pretty strong lady.

BRIAN. Didn't get it from either of us, I can tell you.

MARK. I don't believe that.

BRIAN. Oh dear.

A moment.

Some good news at least. Well done you.

MARK. Thanks. Yeah, I'm over the moon.

BRIAN. Best thing you'll ever do. And the hardest.

MARK. Yeah.

BRIAN. Isn't that right, Ian?

A moment.

IAN. Yeah. Yes.

Silence.

BRIAN. Ian, why are you here?

IAN. What?

BRIAN. Why are you here?

IAN. Brian, let's not start this again. I came to see Andy.

BRIAN. But he's not coming here now. So why are you still here?

IAN. I'm leaving, alright. I just didn't drive so I've got to call a taxi.

BRIAN. And tell them you're going to the hospital.

IAN. What?

BRIAN. Your son is being admitted to hospital.

IAN. I do know that.

BRIAN. You do? You're doing nothing about it. I have to say I'd find that very hurtful, if I was your son.

IAN. It wasn't my choice. I did offer…

BRIAN. If I was your son, I'd find it very hurtful indeed. That my father was five minutes' drive away. And I was in the hospital. And he chose not to see me. On my birthday.

IAN. What am I meant to do? Carol said she didn't want me to go.

MARK. It is the lad's birthday.

IAN. Sorry?

MARK. It's your son's twenty-first.

IAN. It's not quite like that, is it.

MARK. Sorry?

IAN. It's different.

BRIAN. What is?

IAN. With Andy. It's not quite the same, is it?

BRIAN. It is the same instinct, Ian. To protect. And if that instinct isn't screaming at you to get there as soon as you can, to do everything in your power to start making up for everything you've done, if it doesn't make you want to rush up to him and promise him you'll never leave him again, that you'll do anything you can to make him better, then really, really? – you've got no right to call yourself a parent at all.

Silence.

IAN. I'll get a taxi from the end of the road.

BRIAN. And don't just promise him. Promise them. However embarrassing. Promise them.

IAN. Nice to meet you, Mark.

MARK. You too. Good luck. See you again.

IAN. Yes. I hope so.

Bye, Brian.

BRIAN. Promise them.

IAN. Yeah. I will.

IAN *leaves.* MARK *turns to* BRIAN, *impressed.*

MARK. Cometh the hour.

BRIAN. Only for some people. I mean, Carol's a wonderful daughter but when it comes to men she didn't half choose a useless prick.

MARK. I need to keep on the right side of everyone in this family, don't I?

BRIAN. If you know what's good for you.

MARK. Thanks for the warning. Are you sure you're going to be okay here by yourself?

BRIAN. Yeah, just chuck us a paper, that'll keep me busy. I'll do a sudoku. Probably take me till Christmas.

MARK (*passing it to him*). Here you are. You sure you don't need me to stay?

BRIAN. What did you say about keeping on the right side?

MARK. Fine. I'll clear up these then I'll be on my way.

BRIAN. You don't want to check the times?

MARK. No, I'll just rock up. Guilty secret: I like train-station cafés.

MARK *begins to tidy up the glasses as* BRIAN *begins to leaf through the paper.*

BRIAN. I once made love to Patricia on a train.

MARK. Good God.

BRIAN. And we were in our mid-thirties, mind. Not the first flush.

MARK. Good on the pair of you.

BRIAN. Well, it was the sixties. Patricia felt like we were being left behind. Putney to Mortlake. Had to be quick. But in those days that wasn't a problem.

MARK. You should take her on Eurostar.

BRIAN. Trans-Siberian Express more like.

Thing is, I'm lucky. When you've got one you like, why would you want to complicate things? Find one you like, stick with it, hope the gods are with you. Simple. Just luck, I guess. Luck and doggedness. That's all you need. That's all life is. Luck. And doggedness.

During this, MARK *has cleared away the glasses and briefly cleaned the kitchen. He now peers inside* BRIAN's *cake tin. He looks at the message and fathoms the truth.*

MARK. Christ – (*Chuckling.*) women, heh?

BRIAN. And men, mate. And men. Women, men, children. Grandchildren.

All such bloody difficult buggers.

MARK. You sure you'll be alright?

BRIAN. You're lucky I can't get up or I'd…

MARK. I get the message. I'll see you again, Brian.

BRIAN. Be quick then.

MARK. Get away with you.

BRIAN. Very nice to meet you, sir. We need more men in this family. First time I saw you I thought, he'll do. He's got the strength.

MARK. For what?

BRIAN. Carrying my coffin.

MARK. Brian!

BRIAN. Well, God love him, it's not going to be Andy, is it?

MARK (*laughs*). It'd be an honour. Very nice to meet you too, sir.

BRIAN. Take care.

MARK *leaves.*

A long silence. BRIAN *continues to read the paper.*

'The quality of mercy is not strained.
It droppeth as the gentle rain from heaven
Upon the place beneath. It is twice blest:
It blesseth him that give and him that takes.'

Another silence.

The phone rings once, twice, three times, four times, a moment –

Thank you, love.

– five times, six times, the answer machine clicks on.

CAROL (*voice*). This is Carol's. Sorry I'm not here at the moment. Leave a message and I'll get back to you.

CLAIRE (*voice*). Hi, Granddad. It's Claire. / Is Mark still there? Or Dad? Granddad, if you can get to the phone... // (*Starts to cry.*) Um, if you can get to the phone... will you call me?... when you get this... sorry, Granddad... /// um... I'll try later... okay... I love you.

BRIAN. / Claire?

// (*Struggling to get out of his chair.*) Bollocks.

/// Claire?

Claire? God, Claire? Claire.

BRIAN *continues to struggle, eventually falling back in his chair, defeated, close to tears.*

Oh please, oh my Carol, please.

Slow fade to black, as BRIAN *once more begins to try to lift himself from the chair.*

The End.

A Nick Hern Book

The Herd first published in Great Britain as a paperback original in 2013 by Nick Hern Books Limited, The Glasshouse, 49a Goldhawk Road, London W12 8QP, in association with the Bush Theatre, London

The Herd copyright © 2013 Rory Kinnear

Rory Kinnear has asserted his right to be identified as the author of this work

Cover photograph by Eric Richmond
Cover design by Ned Hoste, 2H

Typeset by Nick Hern Books, London
Printed and bound in Great Britain by CPI Group (UK) Ltd

A CIP catalogue record for this book is available from the British Library

ISBN 978 1 84842 334 3